AIRMAN MIS

The True Story of WWII Bomber Pilot John Evans' 114 Days Behind Enemy Lines

BY GREG LEWIS

Contents:

First published in the United Kingdom in 2008 by

Newman Books, 8 Henley Street, Stratford-upon-Avon, Warwickshire CV37 6PT UK
01789 209172 email: newmanbooks@fsmail.net web: http://newmanbooks.blogspot.com

Cover design by Phil Jarrett © 2008

ISBN: 978-0-9558699-0-7

Typeset and printed by

Advertiser Office, Market Place, Easingwold, York YO61 3AB. 01347 821329
email: info@ghsmith.com web: www.ghsmith.com

Preface

In the midnight sky above Belgium, Flight Sergeant John Evans saw the target ahead, lit up by red and green flares.

Adjusting the controls, he turned Halifax HX 334 NP-C and began his bombing run.

The crew tensed. In a moment their bombs would be falling into the darkness below, and they could turn for home.

Their eyes scanned the blackness around their aircraft but they could see nothing.

However, rushing towards them was a war machine every bit as deadly as their own.

John Evans' destiny had been set on a collision course with one of the greatest fighter aces of the Second World War.

Their meeting – as the German raked the four-engine bomber with cannon fire - would deliver John into a new front of the war: one of escape and evasion in Occupied Europe. It was a war which was every bit as dangerous as that of the bomber pilot. A world in which the civilian helpers of the evasion line – the men and women, old and young – faced as high a casualty rate as the fliers they tried to save.

Everyone across Western Europe knew the Allied forces were mounting in England to begin the liberation.

Both the pilots and their helpers just had to stay undetected by the Gestapo and Luftwaffe intelligence long enough for the liberators to arrive.

And so John Evans became the prey in a cat and mouse game which would see him desperately trying to evade capture for 114 nerve-racking days.

Chapter One

The Last Raid

At 2156hrs on May 12, 1944, Halifax HX 334 NP-C lifted off from Lissett, East Yorkshire, and turned towards the coast of Occupied Europe.

At the controls was Flight Sergeant John Evans. He had only been united with his crew a few weeks earlier but already this was to be their 12th bombing mission together over enemy territory.

Plotting the course to the target – the railway marshalling yards at Hasselt in Belgium – was navigator Flying Officer JB "Danny" Daniels.

Wireless operator Sergeant Doug Lloyd was communicating with the outside world as the bomber rose in the night sky over the English coast.

Engineer Sergeant Les Board, rear gunner Flight Sergeant Frank Tait and mid upper gunner Flight Sergeant Dick Colledge – both Australians – would soon be keeping their eyes peeled for enemy fighters.

The key moments for the final member of the crew, Flying Officer Bill "Robbie" Robertson, a Canadian, would come more than two hours after take off as they flew over the marker flares and Robertson released the aircraft's bomb-load.

"We took off at about 10pm and eventually set course over base with twenty two other aircraft," said John Evans. "At the first turning point, Goole, we joined the main bomber stream which consisted of about 150 planes.

"We flew at 6,000ft until we reached the English coast when we climbed to 14,000ft which was our bombing height."

The crew had been lucky so far.

After a long period of training, John had made his first flight at the controls of a Halifax on March 14 while at No 1652 HCU (Heavy Conversion Unit) at Marston Moor, near York. The course required him to become familiar with the plane, doing circuits and landings, fighter affiliation and flying on two or three engines.

At the end of that few short weeks he would finally be united with his aircraft and his crew. They had already been on active duty.

"They had previously been on operational squadron No 158 at Lissett, East Yorkshire, but had lost their original pilot when he was killed flying as a supernumary on a bombing raid in another plane. They had been sent back to Marston Moor to find another pilot."

The bonding had started immediately - in the air and on the ground.

"Betty's Bar in York became a favourite meeting place for aircrew from stations adjacent to the city and was crowded on most nights when ops were not on for one reason or another.

"They came for a welcome evening of relaxation away from the nerve shattering life of constant raids over Germany.

"The beer flowed freely and there was always an abundance of talk and of laughter."

When John was at Marston Moor his brother, Doug, was stationed at Melbourne, Yorkshire, with No 10 Squadron where he was already on bombing operations.

"He and I met at Betty's Bar on a few occasions and enjoyed the fun and games with all the others. He was a pilot on Halifaxes and when I went to No 158 squadron at Lissett we were both in No 4 Group of Bomber Command."

The airfield at Lissett was on the east coast, a few miles south of Bridlington. John and his crew joined No 158 squadron there early in April 1944. Their commanding officer at Lissett was Group Captain Tom Sawyer DFC.

Since the spring of 1943 the numbers of Allied bombing raids had been increasing, with attacks on targets in France and Belgium, as well as in Germany. "Targets such as gun emplacements on the coast, railway marshalling yards and other places of strategic importance were being bombed regularly during the period leading up to the invasion which would take place on June 6," said John, whose first operation was the bombing of a railway yard at Tergnier on April 18. "We were preparing the way."

It was followed by attacks on similar targets at Ottignies, Villeneuve St George and Lens and gun emplacements in the Cherbourg peninsula.

Other raids were also completed including two on German targets – the first on Düsseldorf and the second on Karlsruhe on April 22 and 24 respectively.

"The worst and most daunting (operational flights) were the German targets, Düsseldorf and Karlsruhe, in view of the formidable defence in the Ruhr Valley," he said. "All targets in the Ruhr Valley were difficult ones but thankfully I did just two of them as at the time a lot of the attacks were on strategic targets in France and Belgium such as railway marshalling yards and gun emplacements.

"On approaching Düsseldorf a vast wall of searchlights could be seen long before reaching the target. We had to fly through it to the accompaniment of exploding flak and ever present threat of enemy night-fighters. A most unpleasant experience.

"The master bomber would have identified the target by dropping coloured flares and then would tell us the colour that should be targeted. We came through unscathed and thankfully made our way home.

"The plane could be cold and draughty and very noisy but I don't think it could be called cramped.

"As to fear, well I suppose it varied from person to person but I doubt that anyone could honestly say that he never felt it. It was natural in the circumstances but one just had to press on, which was the term used at the time."

On his eleventh raid John and his crew had switched planes and flown for one time only an aircraft which was to become a legend: 158 Squadron's Halifax NPF or 'Friday the 13th' which would go on to fly an astonishing 128 missions.

The crew's luck, though, would not last. Unlike, 'Friday the 13th' their next raid would be their last.

That twelfth mission was to be to the marshalling yards at Hasselt in Belgium. The date was May 12. Their aircraft that night was Halifax HX 334 NP-C.

"The flight to the target was quiet and without incident. The illuminating flares and the red and green target indicators went down and we made our run in on them.

"Our bombs were released okay and the bomb doors had only been closed for about a minute when it happened and all hell broke loose.

"The gunners must have been keeping a sharp look out but they saw nothing."

The RAF gunners fired machine-gun bullets; the Luftwaffe fighters attacked with two-centimetre cannon shells which were so lethal that a single hit in the fuel tank was enough to bring a bomber down in flames.

Within moments of releasing his bombs, John's life was about to be changed.

The time was 0036hrs on May 13, 1944. At 2,300 metres – 7,500ft – above Hasselt, John and his crew were introduced to Oberleutnant Heinz Wolfgang Schnaufer – the Luftwaffe's greatest night-fighter ace.

Heinz Schnaufer was born on February 16, 1922 at Stuttgart.

He had learned to fly on gliders as a member of a Nationalpolitische Lehranstalt at Potsdam in 1939 and entered the Luftwaffe as a trainee officer-pilot on November 15, 1939.

Following basic military training at Flieger-Ausbildungs-Regiment 42 at Salzwedel, he underwent flying training at Flugzeugführerschule A/B 3 at Guben.

There followed, during 1941, promotion to Leutnant and further training at Flugzeugführerschule C at Alt-Lönnewitz, at Blindflugschule at Schwäbisch Hall and at the Zerstörer-Schule at Wunstorf.

Finally, Schnaufer was posted to night flying school, the Nachtjagdschule 1, based at Schleissheim.

In early November 1941, he was posted to II./NJG 1, based at Stade near Hamburg and then assigned the 5th Staffel of the NJG 1. (A Staffel was the smallest operational unit consisting of about nine aircraft. A Geschwader was the largest, with about ninety.)

On January 15, 1942, II./NJG 1 transferred to St-Trond in Belgium and a month later Schnaufer saw his first operational experience as part of a Luftwaffe escort to the ships Scharnhorst, Gneisenau and Prinz Eugen as they broke out from Brest en-route to Norway.

Luftwaffe aircrew took on secondary responsibilities and, in April, Schnaufer was appointed Technischer Offizier, technical officer, of II./NJG 1. This gave him close contact with the ground personnel, the people who would prepare and repair his aircraft while he slept, and who would cheer him on when he flew up into the skies above them.

Schnaufer first did what he had been trained to on the night of June 1-2, 1942. It would start a grim pattern for the RAF, although his reign of night terror very nearly ended before it began.

His first victim that night was a Halifax four-engine bomber near Leuven in Belgium. But on attacking a second aircraft, his fighter was hit by return fire.

Despite a leg wound, Schnaufer managed to successfully land his damaged aircraft at St-Trond.

He spent most of the rest of the month in hospital. However, his record afterwards is a tribute to his ruthlessness, skill and luck. That first encounter would mark the only time that Schnaufer or one of his crew members would be wounded in aerial combat during the war.

By the end of 1942, he had shot down seven aircraft; twelve months later his total kills stood at 42. By then, he was already a hero. He had shot down three planes in a single night, July 31/August 1, 1942, and been promoted to Oberleutnant in July 1943.

Schnaufer was transferred to IV./NJG 1, based at Leeuwarden in Holland, where he was appointed Staffelkapitän 12./NJG 1, in August 1943 and on New Year's Eve 1943 he was awarded the Ritterkreuz – the Knight's Cross.

On the night of May 12, 1944, he took off from St Trond at 23.56. He was flying a Messerschmitt Bf 110 coded G9+HF. This was not his normal aircraft – historian Wim Govaerts explained that between April and June 1944 he normally flew operations in G9+DF. However, while this would be the only time he would fly in this particular aircraft Schnaufer was more than familiar with the Me 110. This was his 109th operation. As he took off into the night sky, with his crew – radio/radar operator Fritz Rumpelhardt (70 missions) and Wilhelm Gänsler, who had joined as an extra crew member, a look-out - he already had 62 victories under his belt.

By the time he returned to St Trond at 1.25am on the 13th, 89 minutes later, he could claim three more kills, starting with Halifax HX 334 NP-C – John Evans' aircraft.

The second victory, according to Schnaufer himself, was over Londerzeel, eight kilometres west of Mechelen, although the office which logged daily victories recorded it as five kilometres north-east of Balen. Wim Govaerts believes Schnaufer probably shot down Halifax MZ562, of 640 Squadron, which crashed at Balen-Wezel, near the dynamite factory at Poudreries Réunis (de Belgique - PRB). The Londerzeel 'kill' probably belonged to Hans-Heinz Augenstein of 12./NJG 1, according to Govaerts.

Schaufer's third victim of the night is beyond dispute: Halifax LV919, of 466 Squadron, which crashed at Hoogstraten - although Schnaufer noted 'Hoepsteten'.

Whatever details of the German ace's list of victims, in the sky above northern Belgium that night, a burst from his cannons had made John Evans' aircraft uncontrollable.

"The first indication we had that we were being attacked was when cannon fire and tracer bullets came crashing through the fuselage," remembered John.

"The rear gunner must have seen something for he told me to dive to port.

"There was now a huge fire somewhere aft of the engineer and the plane was filled with thick smoke. Nobody appeared to have been hit.

"I had turned to port and was diving when the second burst hit us."

The starboard mainplane was on fire and the aileron control had been rendered useless. The blaze spread quickly through the body of the aircraft.

John shouted his instruction to his crew: "Jump! Jump! Jump!"

Every man acknowledged the skipper and scrambled from his position. Danny, Robbie and Doug left through the forward escape hatch. Les disappeared from his post and John assumed that he had left by the rear escape hatch with the mid upper gunner. (The rear escape hatch was the entrance door to the aircraft and was designated as the emergency escape route for the mid upper gunner and the flight engineer. The rear gunner of a Halifax, in this case Frank Tait, was able to swivel his turret around by 90 degrees and eject through the open door.)

The blaze raging furiously all around him, John then had a heart-stopping moment.

"I saw that my parachute had somehow become dislodged from its housing and was lying right on the edge of the open front escape hatch," he said. "I quickly grabbed it, clipped it to my parachute harness and left through the open escape hatch."

Suddenly John was spinning through the night air.

"When I pulled the release cord the resulting jerk was so violent that I lost one of my flying boots."

On the ground there were only two recorded witnesses to the sickening sight of the airplane spinning in flames to the ground, about 12 kilometres from Hasselt, somewhere between the target and the town of Genk: Unterscharführer Holtermann and Rottenführer Brindöpke, of the 1.Werkstatt Kompanie SS-Panzer Regiment 1 (Leibstandarte Adolf Hitler), who were stationed in the vicinity.

From his spot in the sky, Schnaufer watched the plane's last moments too. He noted in his book of victories – it "crashed burning after one attack".

John Evans was dangling from a canopy of silk watching the same scene.

"On the way down I saw a huge fire erupting in the near distance and knew it was our plane after it had crashed," he said.

He drifted down, Belgium rushing up towards his feet to meet him. His eyes peered into the inky blackness and he had a sudden fear that the country below had an instant and unpleasant shock in store for him.

"As I got nearer to the ground I could make out a large area beneath me which appeared to be darker than the surrounding area and I was fearful that I was going to fall into a lake."

The 'lake' though was the dark of a wood, as he discovered as he went crashing through the tops of a cluster of fir trees.

"The next moment I touched the ground quite gently," he said. "I landed so gently it was like jumping off a chair. After releasing myself from my harness I found that the parachute had caught in the top of one of the trees and had acted as a brake for my fall.

"In the distance a dog was barking and I could hear men shouting so decided to postpone my attempt to release the parachute from the tree in case my efforts made too much noise."

Eventually everything went quiet and John cautiously started to release the parachute.

"It took me about an hour as I was still afraid of making too much noise and the sound of branches when they broke were like pistol shots. However it finally fell to earth and I dug a hole in which to bury it together with my life jacket.

"But before doing so I cut out a piece of silk with my knife to wrap around my foot which was now minus a flying boot."

The crew had baled out at about 12.30am. It was now about 2.30am. The moon had risen and the night was cold. There was nothing John could do now except sit there and wait for the dawn.

"As I sat there I went over all that had happened and hoped and prayed that all the crew were alive and well," he said. "Then my thoughts turned to home and I visualised my parents soon getting a message to say I was missing.

"I knew how sad they would feel, as would my two aunts in Goodwick and my sisters Mair and Enid in Port Talbot. I thought, too, about my brother Cyril in the South African Navy and my other brother Doug who was nearing the end of his operational tour in No 10 squadron. There would now be an additional burden on his shoulders until he had completed his remaining bombing missions."

Chapter Two

Goodwick, the Rockies and Bomber Command

The town of Goodwick lies sheltering in a bay on the west Wales coast, home to a ferry service which has connected passengers with Ireland since the first decade of the 20th Century. Today, the town is dominated by the terminal and the breakwater of Fishguard Harbour, which curves like a crooked finger into the Irish Sea. In fact, it always has been. Although it lies so close to Fishguard, which has a rich history going back to medieval times, Goodwick grew up almost entirely during the nineteenth and twentieth century. While there were houses there in Tudor times, Goodwick really began to develop into what it is today in 1906 when the ferry terminal and railway link from Haverfordwest were opened by the Great Western Railway, the Fishguard and Rosslare Railway, and the City of Cork Steam Packet. It then grew from being a village to a town.

Goodwick then owes much to the sea. And John Evans' family were part of that tradition themselves.

His father was Captain Ben Evans. He worked for Great Western Railway as a tug master at Fishguard Harbour, although he had been born in the village of Trefin, along the coast towards St Davids. His mother, Laura, was born in 1878 to a well-known Goodwick family. Her father, Captain Ben Williams, was lost at sea during a voyage to Australia when she was just six. Another sailor, John's paternal grandfather, Captain John Evans, died in Cardiff in 1892.

Ben and Laura Evans had five children. Cyril in 1904; Mair in 1908; Enid in 1913; John on June 30, 1919 and Doug in 1922.

"Goodwick was transformed from a small quiet village into a very much busier and more important one in the early 1900s when the GWR extended the railway there and built the port from which the cross-channel vessels subsequently operated," said John.

"My memories of growing up there are happy ones. We were a close-knit family with two maiden aunts also living nearby, as well as another uncle and aunt. So there was a lot of inter-visiting as it were.

“The environment was safe and stable and whatever crimes were committed were few and of a minor nature. We were allowed to wander freely with our friends as I remember and to go swimming in the sea without anyone wondering where we were. It was altogether a very carefree existence.

“The influence of the chapel was strong at that time and attendance on Sundays was obligatory. There were five places of worship and they each had their own incumbent.

“I went to Goodwick County Primary School when I was four years old, from where I passed the scholarship when I was 11 and then attended Fishguard County School. The respective headmasters were Mr Evan Anthony and Mr Joseph Jones, both of whom were strict disciplinarians.”

Cyril would go on to become a marine engineer and serve with the Union Castle Line – from Southampton to South Africa – before settling in South Africa in the 1930s. He joined the South African Navy – the Seaward Defence Force – at the outbreak of the Second World War, served in the Mediterranean and was awarded the Distinguished Service Cross. He died in 1959.

Mair and Enid worked for the Post Office and after they married lived not far from each other in Margam outside Port Talbot, south Wales.

In spite of moving far and wide from Goodwick the family remained close.

But the age gap between the children meant that John naturally spent most time with his younger brother Doug – and their affinity continued out of childhood and into their adult lives.

At the outbreak of the war both were living about seventy miles from their home in Swansea, and working for their uncle, Mr G H Cann, at his builders’ merchants business. John was 20 years old.

On October 30, 1939, John went for his medical at the YMCA buildings on St Helen’s Road, Swansea, and on Wednesday, November 15, he presented himself at the Royal Army Service Corps base in Aldershot for basic training. During the next two years, as Hitler’s armies moved through western Europe creating a Greater German Reich, he served at Blackdown, Hampshire; Margate; Ossington, Nottinghamshire; Sutton, Ashfield and Mansfield, where he became an instructor.

John was not the only one in uniform. Cyril had joined up in South Africa, and Doug had signed on with the forces a few months after John – although Doug went straight into the RAF.

"I suppose it was difficult for my parents to see both of us joining up, as well as our brother in South Africa," said John. "But I do not remember them expressing misgivings. It was happening to so many people."

While John was at Mansfield he heard the RAF was seeking volunteers from the army for training as aircrew. "A few of us decided to take the plunge much to the disgust of our commanding officer, a Lieutenant Colonel of the old school, who could not understand why anyone should wish to leave the British army to serve in what was regarded by him as a very junior and less important service," said John, who would become known to all his colleagues in the air force as Jack.

The transfer to the RAF came through on July 21, 1941 and John reported in the first place to Lord's cricket ground in London. The home of cricket had been taken over by the RAF and become the Air Crew Reception Centre (ACRC).

John went through more medical tests and was billeted with the other recruits in requisitioned blocks of flats in St John's Wood. The rooms were entirely empty of furniture and the men slept on mattresses on the floor. For meals they were formed into squads and marched twice a day to the restaurant at nearby London Zoo.

The initial aptitude and medical tests complete, John went to the Initial Training Wing (ITW) at Newquay, Cornwall, for basic training. "We were housed in various hotels that had been requisitioned by the RAF and one of the members of my flight was Max Jaffa who later became famous as a violinist and orchestra leader. Our training involved drill and physical training as well as classroom work in Morse code, aircraft recognition, navigation and other subjects."

Basic training complete, it was on to No 22 EFTS (Elementary Flying Training School) at Marshall's Airfield, Cambridge. "This was our introduction to flying," he said. "The planes in use were Tiger Moths (DH 82s), a small light and easy to fly bi-plane, and my first flight with an instructor was on October 1, 1941."

Eleven days later, he flew solo for the first time. He had had only eight hours instruction.

"I do remember flying solo for the first time and I see from my log book that it took 10 minutes," he stated. "As to my feelings well I suppose there were a few butterflies but mainly a sense of relief that an important milestone had been successfully passed. It just involved taking off then doing a circuit of the airfield and landing. It had been practised many times so was really no big deal, although I remember that some students failed to make it for one reason or another and sadly were taken off the course. This also happened at every stage of training, of course."

There was now further training in night-flying, emergency action, aerobatics, instrument flying and forced landings. Classroom studies continued too, in the theory of flight, the rules of flying, aircraft recognition, the working of the aircraft engine and controls. Recruits were also required to attain a certain standard of competence in transmitting messages by Morse code.

The night-flying took place from a field at Caxton Gibbet, near Cambridge. "The flare path used was a rudimentary affair lined with what were known as goose-neck flares," remembered John. "Solo flying involved taking off, making a circuit of the field and then landing and it was the practice to allow the aircraft navigation lights to remain on in view of the inexperience of the trainee pilots.

"In those days German hit-and-run intruder planes sometimes came in over the east coast at night to attack airfields and aircraft landing and taking off there."

If a warning was received at Caxton Gibbet that intruders had been detected in the area the pilots of any planes in the air were warned by a flashing Aldis lamp and ordered to land immediately. The flare path lights were then extinguished.

"One night the warning was received and the established procedure was put into action but one trainee pilot had drifted some way from the airfield and failed to see the flashing Aldis lamp.

"His first warning of trouble was when bullets came crashing through the fuselage and, realising that he was being attacked, he reacted with commendable presence of mind and switched off his navigation lights immediately.

"Fortunately neither he nor the engines and controls had been hit and he remained in control and continued to make circular flights of where he thought the airfield to be.

"The intruder eventually disappeared, the flare path lights came on again and the trainee pilot, although he had been flying in total darkness, found more by good luck than good judgement, that he was not too far away.

"The Aldis lamp picked him out and he was able to come in and land.

NATIONAL SERVICE (ARMED FORCES) ACT, 1939

ENLISTMENT NOTICE

MINISTRY OF LABOUR AND NATIONAL SERVICE
EMPLOYMENT EXCHANGE,

EMPLOYMENT EXCHANGE,
NORTHAMPTON LANE,
SWANSEA

Date 10 NOV 1939

Mr. John Haggar Evans.
18 Brunswick St.
Swansea.

YOU SHOULD TAKE THIS NOTICE WITH YOU WHEN YOU REPORT

Registration No. SWS. 1153.

DEAR SIR,

In accordance with the National Service (Armed Forces) Act, 1939, you are called upon for service in the TERRITORIAL ARMY and are required to present yourself on WEDNESDAY day 15 NOV 1939 19......, at 10 a.m., or as early as possible thereafter on that day, to :—

1st Training Centre RASC.
Aldershot.
ALDERSHOT. (nearest railway station).

Delete if not applicable ~~A Travelling Warrant for your journey is enclosed. Before starting your journey you must exchange the warrant for a ticket at the booking office named on the warrant. If possible, this should be done a day or two before you are due to travel.~~

A Postal Order for 4s. in respect of advance of service pay, is also enclosed. Uniform and personal kit will be issued to you after joining H.M. Forces. Any kit that you take with you should not exceed an overcoat, change of clothes, stout pair of boots, and personal kit, such as razor, hair brush, tooth brush, soap and towel.

Immediately on receipt of this notice, you should inform your employer of the date upon which you are required to report for service.

Yours faithfully,

D. W. RICHARDS

Manager.

N.S. 12 (4884) Wt. 27800—8813 9/39 B.W. 677

John Evans is called up to the army in November 1939.

"On inspection it was found that there were numerous bullet holes in the plane some of which were very close to where he had been sitting.

"Truly a case of beginner's luck."

During his time at Cambridge John was in civilian billets with Mr and Mrs Wilderspin and their family in Girton Road. "They were very kind to me and I enjoyed my stay with them." Mr Wilderspin worked in the PYE radio factory in the town.

The course at Cambridge ended on January 17, 1942, after a total of 122 hours flying and after a brief period at No 17 EFTS, Peterborough, John learned that he was to go overseas for the next part of his training.

"One's final destination was never divulged in those days for security reasons and airmen were sent to the port of departure not knowing if they were going to Canada, USA, South Africa or Rhodesia," he stated. "However clues were sometimes provided such as whether or not tropical kit had been issued prior to departure."

John's destination was to be Canada. He sailed in an American troopship from the Clyde in a convoy destined for New York in March 1942.

It would be a nervous voyage. The convoy's first escort was to be a small number of British destroyers. They were widely scattered, a fact which combined with knowledge of the intense U-Boat activity in the north Atlantic made the passengers extremely concerned.

"However, after two days or so we rendezvoused with another much larger American convoy coming, so we were told, from Iceland," said John. "Our enlarged convoy now had a very big escort, including the American battleship USS New York, two cruisers and several smaller vessels.

"Every day planes were catapulted from the cruisers to make search for U-Boats and, a day or two before reaching New York, US Navy airships known as blimps would arrive for surveillance purposes. With this massive protection we felt completely safe from the U-Boat threat."

At last the convoy sailed into New York harbour, a most memorable experience.

"It was a sunny day with a clear blue sky and everyone looked out for the Statue of Liberty which duly came into view. The Manhattan skyline too was very impressive."

They left the ship and boarded a train. They were still unsure where their journey might finally end.

Their destination turned out to be Moncton, New Brunswick, which had become a big dispersal centre for RAF personnel from England on their way to training stations in Canada and USA.

John's brother, Doug, had also joined up for aircrew training back in England. He had guessed that John had probably gone to Canada but John had no idea his brother might head there too.

One morning John was standing in the NAAFI queue when he heard a voice saying: "Hullo, John."

He turned to find Doug at his side. "We were overjoyed to see each other and had such a lot to talk about but unfortunately were not together very long before we had to go our separate ways."

Doug went to Georgia for training under the Arnold Scheme and John went to Alberta in western Canada.

Before that, while still at Moncton, John came across a Mr Davies who worked for New Brunswick Department of Agriculture. Mr Davies, who was of Welsh origin, sent an invitation to the camp asking for any Welsh airmen to come to his home for tea.

"I duly went and received a very warm welcome from Mr Davies and his wife. Then came the big surprise. To my astonishment he introduced himself as a Welshman who many years previously had emigrated to Canada from a little village called Goodwick in Pembrokeshire, and he was amazed when I told him that was also my home village.

"Apparently he and a friend called Watkins had cycled down to the Fishguard area from the Rhondda in South Wales when they were young men to look for work on the farms.

"Mr Davies lived in Goodwick and worked locally for a short period before deciding to take the big step of emigrating to Canada. Mr Watkins stayed and remained in farming locally, eventually occupying a farm near Fishguard.

"As his stay in Goodwick was comparatively short Mr Davies did not remember the names of people living there in his day except one – Dai Shem Morgan – who was a very well known character in the village in my young days.

ITW at New Quay in Cornwall, 1941. John Evans is fourth from the left in the third row. The man sixth from the right in the same row is Max Jaffa, later a famous violinist.

"I visited the Davies' several times but my letters after the war remained unanswered and I lost touch with them."

John was only in Moncton for about ten days before he was part of a group which joined the Canadian Pacific Railway train destined for Calgary in Alberta.

The journey took five days and nights, with stops en route at Winnipeg, Brandon and Regina where, John remembered, "groups of well-wishers always seemed to appear to ply us with tea, cakes, coffee and biscuits".

At Calgary the group learned that its destination was to be the RAF station at Penhold, near Red Deer, Alberta, which was known as No 36 SFTS (Service Flying Training Station).

Here the recruits flew twin-engine Airspeed Oxfords. John first flew one with an instructor on April 28, 1942. He completed his first solo flight on May 2.

The recruits again went through a range of disciplines, including night and cross-country flying, low flying, emergency action, navigation and flying on one engine. “Any pupil who failed to reach the required standard during any phase of the course was taken off and sent for retraining as a navigator or bomb aimer.”

John’s instructor was Pilot Officer Peter Horsley, later Air Marshall Peter Horsley.

When out on their own the pilots often took unauthorised risks such as unsupervised low flying.

“And as we were not far from the foothills of the Rockies a visit there just to experience the effects of the terrific up-draughts was often made without the knowledge of our commanding officers. The planes were quite small and the effects were quite violent as I remember.

“It was just a bit of daring that would have been frowned on by our superiors had they known. I was not aware of any possible danger but then we were young and inexperienced. And there was certainly no damage done.

“Had we been found out a severe reprimand would have been the least of our punishment.”

Training might have been similar but life in general in Canada was very different from that of wartorn Britain. “Food was plentiful and the wartime restrictions that we had become used to were all absent. In fact one hardly realised that there was a war on.”

John completed his course successfully at Penhold and was awarded his wings on August 14.

“It had been a gruelling course and I was very aware of a sense of achievement in that at last I had become a fully fledged pilot,” he stated. “The end of the course also meant the parting of the ways with so many friends who had been with me now for several months. Many were sent back to England for posting to bomber squadrons and I was disappointed to learn that I had been selected for an instructors’ course at the RAF station at Vulcan, Alberta.

“I wished to return to England too, little realising how different life was to be on an operational squadron there compared to that in safe, carefree Canada.”

Having been given leave John and two friends decided to spend it in Vancouver. “We travelled by train from Calgary through the Rockies via Banff and Lake Louise and enjoyed the most spectacular scenery with the railway following the course of the Fraser river for a part of the way.

“In Vancouver we were introduced to some expatriate English people, who were extremely kind to us. They provided us with accommodation, showed us around, took us on many trips by car and boat and generally gave us a very pleasant time."

Leave over, they travelled to Vulcan to start yet another course. John was there from September 9 to November 26 before qualifying on a plane called the Cessna Crane. His next move was to training stations at Carberry, Manitoba and Weyburn, Saskatchewan, where he was a staff pilot involved in the instruction of trainee navigators.

By the start of June, 1943, John had been in Canada for over a year. Then he learned he was to return to Britain. He travelled back to Moncton on June 2, 1943, then on June 24, he was taken by train to Halifax, Nova Scotia, where he and others boarded the 'Louis Pasteur' to cross the Atlantic.

The 'Louis Pasteur' was a pre-war French transatlantic liner which like the 'Queen Mary' was so fast that it was safer for them to travel alone rather than in a convoy. Their great speed together with the improved U-Boat detection equipment then available meant that they could quickly take avoiding action when danger threatened. The voyage was completed without incident and they arrived in Liverpool on June 30, John's 24th birthday.

John now found himself at a holding unit at Harrogate and billeting at the Majestic Hotel. Here, John's commanding officer was Squadron Leader LEG Ames, the former Kent and England wicket keeper. (John said Ames was already a famous figure but he was also distant and he does not recall meeting him.)

He was there for a month before going to No 14 Advanced Flying Unit at Banff and Fraserburgh in Scotland where he was reintroduced to the Oxford and where the training consisted mainly of cross country flying, standard beam approach and instrument and night flying. "We were in a very pleasant if remote part of Scotland." He was there for about two months.

At last, John was reaching the final stages of his training as a bomber pilot. He was sent to No 18 OTU (Operational Training Unit) at Worksop where he flew a Wellington bomber for the first time.

"Unfortunately the planes in use were old and had seen better days," he recalled. "Many had been on operational squadrons but were now regarded as fit only for training.

"The unreliability of the aircraft coupled with the inexperience of pilots resulted in a number of crashes in which whole crews were wiped out.

The crew that took off in Halifax HX 334 on the night of May 12, 1944. Back Row: (left to right) Dick Colledge, Mid Upper Gunner; Doug Lloyd, Wireless Operator; "Danny" Daniels, Navigator; Frank Tait, Rear Gunner. Front Row: (l to r) Les Board, Flight Engineer; John Evans, Pilot; Bill "Robbie" Robertson, Bomb Aimer.

YEAR 1944		AIRCRAFT		PILOT, OR 1ST PILOT	2ND PILOT, PUPIL OR PASSENGER	DUTY (INCLUDING RESULTS AND REMARKS)
MONTH	DATE	Type	No.			
—	—	—	—	—	—	— TOTALS BROUGHT FORWARD
APR.	17	HALIFAX III	LK850	F/O CHANT.	SELF.	CIRCUITS.
"	17.	HALIFAX III	LK850.	SELF	CREW.	CIRCUITS.
"	18	HALIFAX III	V.	SELF.	CREW.	LOCAL.
	18	HALIFAX III	H.	SELF.	CREW.	OPS – TERGNIER.
"	20.	HALIFAX III	A.	SELF.	CREW.	OPS – OTTIGNIES.
"	22.	HALIFAX III	E.	SELF.	CREW.	OPS – DUSSELDORF.
"	24.	HALIFAX III	E.	SELF.	CREW.	OPS – KARLSRUHE.
						LANDED AT FOULSHAM
"	25	HALIFAX III	E.	SELF	CREW.	FROM FOULSHAM.
"	26.	HALIFAX III	E.	SELF.	CREW.	OPS – VILLENEUVE. ST GEORGE
"	27.	HALIFAX III	E.	SELF.	CREW.	OPS – AULNOYE.
"	30.	HALIFAX III	E.	SELF.	CREW.	OPS – ACHERES.

The crew's earlier missions during April 1944 are recorded in John's log book.

YEAR 1944.		AIRCRAFT		PILOT, OR 1ST PILOT	2ND PILOT, PUPIL OR PASSENGER	DUTY (INCLUDING RESULTS AND REMARKS)
MONTH	DATE	Type	No.			
—	—	—	—	—	—	— TOTALS BROUGHT FORWARD
MAY	8.	HALIFAX III	B.	SELF.	CREW.	OPS – MARSELINES.
"	10	HALIFAX III	A.	SELF.	CREW.	"Y" CROSS COUNTRY.
"	10.	HALIFAX III	F.	SELF.	CREW.	OPS – LENS.
"	12	HALIFAX III	C	SELF	CREW	OPS – MAFFELT. (HASSELT)
						MISSING.
					SHOT DOWN BY E.A. OVER TARGET.	
					EVADED CAPTURE. SPENT 4½ MONTHS IN	
					OCCUPIED TERRITORY. REACHED ENGLAND SEPT 4th	

Another page of John's log book shows his flight at the controls of 158 Squadron's famous F, 'Friday the 13th', Halifax on May 10, 1944, and the fateful mission to Hasselt two days later, after which he and the crew were posted missing.

Mijnheer and Mevrouw Buntinx, the Flemish farming couple who first gave John Evans shelter. This photograph was taken just before the war.

When John Evans approached this farm soon after being shot down he did not know if he would find friend or foe. Fortunately, the Buntinx family who lived there had connections to the Belgian resistance movement.

“I remember being told that the Wellingtons had all been on ops and were all clapped out but I do not remember who told me this or whether there was any truth in it. However, I do remember attending a morale boosting meeting called by the Commanding Officer on the subject.”

In peacetime a great scandal would have erupted but in wartime, of course, it was all kept quiet and no information was allowed to leak out.

“Morale was very low but complaints were not entertained and the old motto ‘Press on Regardless’ applied.”

Bomber crews, though, were now taking shape. “We now teamed up with navigators, wireless operators, engineers and gunners to form makeshift crews for training purposes and our last flight was a leaflet dropping raid on Argentan in France to give us, I suppose, a taste of things to come.”

Every pilot awaits the moment he is united with his plane and his crew.

John Evans’ transfer came, and he left Worksop for No 1652 HCU (Heavy Conversion Unit) at Marston Moor, near York, for conversion on to four-engine Halifax bombers.

His first flight on a Halifax was on March 14 and this course mainly required him to become familiar with the plane, doing circuits and landings, fighter affiliation and flying on two or three engines. “It was here that I teamed up with my final crew. They had previously been on operational squadron No 158 at Lissett, East Yorkshire, but had lost their original pilot when he was killed flying as a supernumary on a bombing raid in another plane. They had been sent back to Marston Moor to find another pilot.”

And so John joined his crew, a mix of Australian, English, Welsh and Canadian: “Danny”; “Robbie”; Doug; Les; Frank and Dick.

Chapter Three

First Hours, May 13th 1944

Sitting in the dark wood, with the sun slowly rising, John thought about all that had gone before.

But one thing he never considered was giving himself up. Neither did he want to get caught which, as the sun rose, became an ever more likely fate.

Just after daylight broke a German spotter plane flew low over the woods, scouring the area for survivors of the raiding force. Without a doubt it would have spotted John's parachute if he had not retrieved and buried it.

"I now had to decide what to do next but had no idea what direction to take. I obviously had to try to find someone to help me if possible but realised what a dangerous undertaking that might turn out to be.

"Suddenly the sound of men singing came to my ears and it seemed to be only a short distance away. I decided to go and investigate and cautiously made my way through the undergrowth in the direction of the singing and after walking about a hundred yards came to a lane.

"I peeped out from behind a bush and had the shock of my life to see a squad of German soldiers with rifles on their shoulders marching toward me and still singing at the tops of their voices. Incidentally it was very good singing. "I ducked down behind the bush hardly daring to breathe and scared stiff that one of them would spot me as they passed.

"However they carried on and I just sat down to recover from the shock."

After a short time John decided to walk along the edge of the wood, keeping the lane in view until he saw someone who looked as if he might be able to help.

After about ten minutes he came to a crossroads and could see a man coming towards him on a bicycle.

"As he got nearer I could see that he was some sort of farm labourer or land worker and decided to stop him and ask for help. I left the bushes and walked into the road in front of him, then signalled him to stop which he did immediately.

"I must have looked rather wild in my dirt stained battle dress and the white piece of silk wrapped around my foot because as soon as he saw me a scared look came to his face, and I am certain he thought I was going to rob him. "Before he had a chance to say anything I told him in some broken French that I had learned in school that I was an English airman, that I had baled out and landed in the woods and asked him if he could help me.

"He looked at me dumbly as if he didn't understand. I then asked him if he could speak French and, although he probably could, he shook his head violently and started to talk volubly in Flemish.

"I decided that he was not worth bothering with any further so said 'Bon jour' and carried on down the road.

"I had only gone about twenty yards when he called me back and pointing in the direction that I was going uttered one word 'Boches' and then he pointed down one of the other roads indicating that I should go in that direction after which he got on his cycle and pedalled quickly away.

"While my school French – which would come in handy later – had had no effect on the first person I'd accosted, it is amazing how much you can get away with gestures when the occasion demands."

That stranger in the countryside, with whom he shared only one word, would be the first of many who would keep the Welshman out of harm's way.

John now followed a lane which had the wood on one side and fields on the other. There were deep cart tracks on either side of the lane but it did not look as if it was used very much.

After twenty minutes a small farmhouse with two stone chimneys came into view. John hid behind a bush to watch for some signs of activity. When nobody entered or left the farm during the next half an hour he decided to risk showing himself again.

"I tapped on the door and after a few minutes a woman carrying a baby opened it. I immediately told her my tale of woe and without saying a word she went back into the kitchen and called her husband. When he came I repeated my story and he asked me to come inside.

"There were seven children seated around a table in the kitchen, the oldest one looked about fifteen. The farmer asked me to sit down and they all stared at me without saying anything."

The farmer, a Flemish man named Buntinx, with a balding head and a small, neat moustache, could speak a little French and he began to fire questions at John who could see his host was concerned that the visitor was who he said he was and was not a German spy. John took out his escape kit, his maps and money, and seemed finally to convince him that he was a genuine RAF airman.

Mijnheer and Mevrouw (Mr and Mrs) Buntinx gave John a bowl of very dark coffee and a piece of black sticky bread with a slice of fatty bacon on top. He then said he was going to fetch someone who could speak English and who would help.

"I was naturally not quite sure that he himself was 'on the level' so I kept a good look-out through the window in case he came back with a few Germans in which case I was going to make a bolt for it.

"When he did come back he brought with him a young man who looked to be about 21 years of age. He could speak English reasonably well and, after asking me some more questions, said that he would go and fetch someone who would get me back to England, and that in the meantime I could go in to the barn and sleep for a few hours. This I agreed to do gladly.

"I do not now remember what the men from the resistance asked me but whatever it was they were satisfied as to my identity. They had to be very careful as the crafty Germans had the habit of trying to infiltrate the escape lines by one of their men pretending to be an airman evading capture."

The young man who had questioned John was named Jaak Cardinaels, although John would not know this for many years to come. He was, in fact, only 16 but had already been working for the resistance under his chief, Mijnheer Vander Biest, for two years.

The farmer had got John help but he still had a shock in store for the airman. At 4pm he woke John up and brought him down into the kitchen.

"Imagine my surprise when I saw none other than Robbie seated there as large as life. He had been brought there by another farmer. It made us both feel very much better to have each other's company.

"The farmer said that he was going to take us to a hut about half a kilometre away and that we were to stay there until some men came for us."

Chapter Four

On The Run, May 13 to May 28

At the time John Evans was shot down Belgium had been under occupation for four years, ever since the German army had rolled in to the country on May 10, 1940.

While its people had become part of the Greater German Reich, its skies had become filled with bombers. The flight paths created by the huge bomber forces which left Britain to fly over north-west Europe meant Belgium would become a focus for evasion line activity.

Thousands of airmen were to bail out and crash land over Belgium and Holland.

Once down, they would only survive if they made contact with a friendly person who could help them escape the attentions of the Germans.

Work on the evasion lines was incredibly hazardous, involving the creation of a network which reached from Belgium through France to the Spanish border. This meant that people who hardly knew each other were forced to trust each other, that couriers had to accompany airman – carrying false identity papers and not speaking a word of anything but English – on long journeys through occupied territory and that everyone lived with the ever-present danger of being given away, accidentally or by betrayal. According to Michael Moores LeBlanc in his essay on Escape & Evasion History on the 100th Bomb Group website (www.100thbg.com), it was the most "dangerous kind of resistance activity" of the war. "It is said that two 'helpers' died for every Allied airman who was successfully evacuated - this does not count those who were arrested and sent to concentration camps but survived to come home broken in body and in spirit.

"No 'helper' could expect to operate, and history was to prove it, for more than six months. Many, very many, did not last even half that long."

At the heart of this hugely dangerous clandestine world was the Comète Line, the evasion line celebrated by the hugely popular BBC series of the 1970s, Secret Army. It was to suffer many betrayals and mass arrests but was to survive until the liberation of Belgium in September 1944. (It had been founded in 1941 by a woman, Andrée de Jong or Dedee, who was eventually arrested but survived incarceration in Ravensbrück concentration camp.)

With thousands of men who were not in essential occupations being conscripted as forced labour for the Third Reich, many Comète guides, couriers and keepers of safe houses were women. Those without children – including couples – or the elderly kept the best safe houses as they had no young children to give them away accidently. Less than one in five of those who were arrested and sent to camps were to survive to return to their homes in peacetime.

The hunt for the evasion lines had began in January 1942 when Herman Goering was made aware of their existence and ordered the Abwehr, the German army intelligence service, to destroy them. The following month, Nazi commanders in France and Belgium ordered that hiding or assisting Allied personnel would be punishable by death.

The Comète Line was to be twice infiltrated by a Nazi agent named Jacques Desoubri, who actually forced it to close for a time in January 1944.

However, around the same time the number of Allied bombing raids over Europe dramatically increased as plans were made for the Second Front. With more aircrews to deal with, the lines became stretched, forcing locals to keep aircrew fed, watered and safe in Belgium without passing them down the line.

Although it would receive financial help from MI9 – the British intelligence department charged with training aircrew in the skills of escape and evasion - the Comète remained a proudly independent Belgian organization. It helped 800 Allied soldiers and aircrew to reach freedom.

Many airman, like John, would pass from the resistance, the White Army, the Armée Blanche, to the Comète Line.

The Ardennes Forest of eastern Belgium and northern France really became central to the evasion line activity in May 1944, when organisers became concerned that any attempt to liberate Brussels following the coming invasion would result in a long siege of the city. Fearing that the downed airmen would become trapped in increasingly unsafe urban hideouts (and encouraged by MI9's Airey Neave), the helpers scattered hundreds of airmen into camps throughout the thick forest.

John and Robbie sat in the Buntinx hut for about an hour. They had one thing in particular on their mind: "Neither of us knew anything about the remainder of the crew."

Then the hut door opened and five men came in. They saluted the RAF men and one of them who could speak a little English said that they were members of the Belgium White Army and that they were going to help.

"They provided us with overalls, caps and boots and a cycle each. After we had put on this new clothing we were given our instructions.

"One man – the one who could speak English – was to go on in front and Robbie and I were to follow him on our cycles at a distance of 100 yards."

The sun was very strong and with all of the extra clothing the cyclists quickly became very warm. They rode for about thirty minutes before coming to the village at Zonhoven.

The guide turned into a garden which led to the back of a house. John and Robbie followed him and inside the house introduced to his wife and sister-in-law. "They seemed very pleased to see us and straight away put some food in front of us," John remembered.

As they ate hungrily, the guide told the two airmen that they would stay in the house only until 10pm that night. Then he would take them to a hideout in some woods where they would live for a short while with five Russian prisoners. The Russians had been forced to work in local Belgian coal mines until they escaped from the captivity of their prison camp.

John recalled their movements that night well.

"Shortly before 10 o'clock we set out once again on our bicycles with the guide in front and Robbie and I following at a distance of about 100 yards," he said. "After cycling for 30 minutes we stopped and the guide explained that we would have to hide our bicycles in the bushes and go the rest of the way on foot.

"We were now at the edge of a wood. It was getting dusk and in the wood it was quite dark. The guide told us to remain where we were and he went on ahead: when he whistled, we were to follow. A very short while later we heard his whistle and went in that direction."

They found the guide standing with a tall, well-dressed and very distinguished looking man. This was 'The Baron', a genuine nobleman who lived in a castle close by called Kasteel Vogelsanck. His full name was Baron De Villenfagne. He spoke English very well, and got by in German and Russian too.

He took over now, surprising John and Robbie by telling them that they would be taken to a little "house under the ground". They would be there for a few days and then be taken to Hasselt.

Now they headed on through the wood, walking for an hour before coming to a small river. On one side of the river was a steep bank.

The Baron stopped and, putting his fingers to his lips, made a short, sharp whistle. Immediately, a piece of turf in the bank was thrown aside revealing a hole. There was movement and the completely bald head of a Russian appeared. This was the Capitaine and he had been appointed a sort of head man by The Baron. The Russians reaction to the new arrivals was one of complete delight. That was obvious in their faces and their body language, although full communication was a problem. They got by because one of the Russians, called Michele, could speak a little French and so could the two RAF men.

"They were very kind and just couldn't do enough for us," said John. "Apart from cooking all our food, one of them acted as barber and shaved us every day. They also shared with us their tobacco and cigarettes and wouldn't listen to any refusal."

On the second day in the hut John and Robbie had a major shock when the Baron arrived first with Doug Lloyd and later with the navigator Danny and engineer Les. "We were of course delighted to see each other and once more spent a long time swapping experiences."

The Baron and his helpers – a forester named Louis Wouters and 16-year-old René Jaspers who lived with his parents in Zonhoven - were the fugitives' link to the outside world.

They visited regularly, always bringing food and tobacco from their own meagre supplies and the latest world news. Everyone was eagerly awaiting the Second Front, wondering when the Allies would launch the invasion of France.

"One day one of the Baron's men brought some civilian clothes along and they were sorted out as best we could - according to size." John's fitted reasonably well but Doug's were much too small and Robbie's were not ideal either.

But ill-fitting clothes were far from the only worry during that week they spent in the wood.

"Occasionally a stranger would be seen in the woods or approaching it and then we always had to dive into the dug-out and pull the cover over the entrance," said John.

The Russians had put together an efficient sentry system and always saw anyone approaching a long time before they reached the camp.

For the most part life in the wood was tedious and uncomfortable. "We used to play cards to while away the time but even so it went very slowly," said John. "A lot of it was spent in conversation with Michele. It appeared that he had been a student in Kiev University before the war and had been captured by the Germans during their last attempt to reach Moscow."

The unselfish Russians had insisted the RAF men occupy the underground accommodation while they slept above in the open air.

They would all go to bed at about 10pm and not get up before 8am so a great deal of their time was spent asleep.

Now kitted out in civilian clothes, the three downed airmen – Doug Lloyd, John Evans and Bill "Robbie" Robertson hide in the woods at Vogelsanck. The picture was taken by René Jaspers, who would later be sent to a concentration camp.

Hiding out among the bushes and trees in the woods at Vogelsanck are (standing) five escaped Russian prisoners of war and the RAF airmen Doug Lloyd, Bill Robertson and, wearing the hat, John Evans.

“The so-called bed was just a mound of earth covered with ferns and straw on which the three of us had to sleep much to our mutual discomfort,” John said. “It was impossible to turn oneself without waking the other two, especially if you occupied the middle position. However we were thankful that we were there and not in a prison camp.

“The food consisted mainly of soup (made from cubes), potatoes, black bread and jam. Le Capitaine was quite an expert at making coffee from some special berries which he used to collect in the woods. Frankly, I much preferred ordinary water.”

Sunday, May 20, was John’s eighth and final day in the makeshift camp under the trees.

“On that day the Baron arrived with another man – a small, dark-haired, pale-faced man -whom he informed us would take us to Hasselt on the first stage of our journey home,” John stated.

“We had to walk for about an hour through the woods until we came to where the bicycles were. After having been given instructions we mounted our machines and set off.”

The new guide, M Biernaux, went out in front. John followed at 100 yards, with Doug and Robbie another 100 yards behind their skipper. (The other two crew members were separated from John again, and went on to hide in different safe houses.) The cyclists were travelling along a busy road. They could move quickly but it was a gamble, a risk, and it was one which looked likely to end in disaster.

“We were travelling along the main road when we had our first real fright,” John explained. “A motorcycle combination carrying two German soldiers came toward us and passed by. They then turned back and passed us again, and when they reached the bend in the road they once more turned and came towards us.

“We were quite scared by now and were convinced that they suspected us. “On drawing level with Doug and Robbie the motorcycle screeched to a stop. We thought, ‘Well, this is it now’, expecting to hear shouts.

“But nothing happened and when we looked back we could see that there was something wrong with the motorcycle. One of the Germans was kneeling down and tinkering with the engine.

“What a relief! The remainder of the journey to Hasselt passed without incident, although we did see many Germans and the town itself seemed to be well-stocked with them. We were living constantly on our nerve ends.

“Biernaux’s house was in one of the main streets and, although there were many Germans in the vicinity, he instructed us to leave our bicycle outside and come in through the front door."

Florent and Olympe Biernaux had quite a large house at 16 Boulevard Thonissen, and in a smart, airy, ground floor room, they were introduced to two Canadians who had also been shot down. "One of them had rather a severe wound in his right thigh and was being kept in the house until it was quite better."

The food was better and more plentiful here, thanks to M Biernaux's connections to the Black Market – a source which also enabled M Biernaux to get medicine for John: "Shortly before leaving the woods I drank some water from a nearby brook. The water must have been contaminated because a violent stomach upset ensued causing sickness which stayed with me to some degree for a long time."

For all its comforts, though, Hasselt was something the wood was not, as John and his crew knew only too well: it was a target for Allied air raids.

"The day after we arrived the Americans sent over some Thunderbolt fighters to dive bomb the bridge across the Albert Canal which runs through Hasselt," said John.

"They had no opposition except for some very light flak but failed to hit the bridge."

The men watched the raids from Biernaux's backyard for three days.

On the Wednesday morning (May 25), Biernaux said he was taking them to Liège.

"There was quite a queue when we got to the tram stop including a number of German soldiers who looked as if they were going on leave," said John. "We managed to get four seats together and Biernaux, of course, bought the tickets. We naturally were unable to say a word during the journey as our language would have given us away.

"At Tongres we had to change trams so the process of trying to stick together and looking as natural as possible began all over again.

"This tram was very crowded and we had to stand. Biernaux once again bought the tickets. We eventually arrived in the main square in Liège and Biernaux took us to a café close by and gave us a glass of beer."

The RAF men waited anxiously as Biernaux went to make a phone call.

"After about fifteen minutes a man and girl came in and were greeted by Biernaux. They talked for a while and then Biernaux told us that we would now go with these new friends. He wished us good luck, said goodbye and left."

Again, a new guide gave them instructions to follow. The guide started off across the square. As he walked, John looked to his left where there was a large building bearing the word 'Oberfeldkomdantur' in huge letters. The building's entrance was guarded by German sentries.

They reached the other end of the square and dipped down a street.

The guide turned around and said in good English: "Do you see those two men in front, one of them wearing a grey overcoat?" The airmen nodded. "Well, follow them. Bon chance."

John, Doug and Robbie followed the next guides into a side street. The two men quickly stopped at a door and motioned the others to enter. The airman went inside, followed by the guides.

They all ran up a flight of stairs and found themselves in a tailor's shop. There, they found three more men. When they spoke, John was surprised to find they were American airmen. They were living there for the time being.

"It gave us courage to think that we were not the only ones having to go through this," said John.

The shop was the headquarters of the escape organisation in Liège. While there John met several Belgians who acted as guides.

They were fed and told they would be taken that afternoon to another temporary home – John thought of them all as 'billets' – although, firstly, they would be having their photographs taken for identity cards.

"These were taken in a studio in one of the main streets after which we walked for about one-and-a-half hours before reaching our destination," said John. "This proved to be another tailor's shop."

Now the crew members would be split again. The next morning Robbie was taken away by a guide and, later in the day, another man came to fetch John and Doug.

"We travelled for a while on the tram and were eventually handed over to another man who took us to our new billet," John explained. "The house stood at the corner of two fork roads and was in one of the busiest parts of Liège.

"Madame Marchoul and her daughter seemed delighted to see us and straight away prepared a meal and afterwards showed us where we were to sleep."

John and Doug were staying on the fifth floor and their room had a great view of everything going on in the street. They could also see right into the grounds of the convent across the other side of the road – although it was not nuns they found themselves watching.

"This convent had been taken over by the Germans and was being used as a barracks," said John. "We often watched them sunbathing on the lawns.

Bill "Robbie" Robertson, Doug Lloyd and John Evans photographed in the garden of the house at Boulevard Thonissen in Hasselt where they were kept safe during their second week on the run.

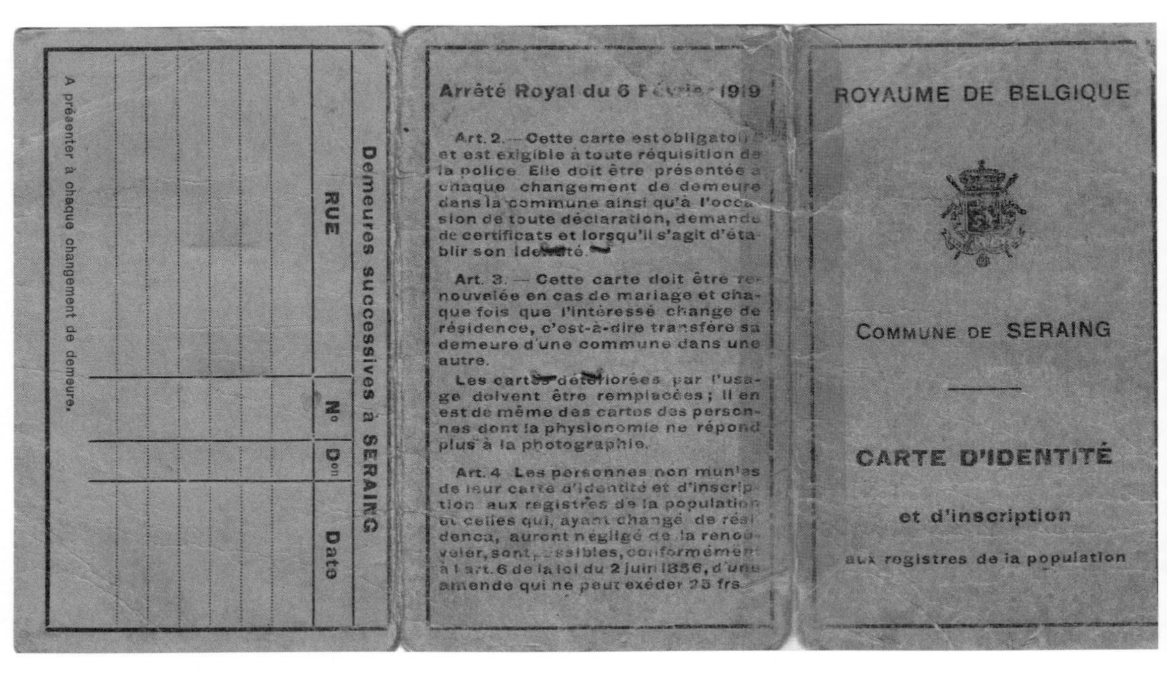

Demeures successives à SERAING

RUE	N°	D^on	Date

A présenter à chaque changement de demeure.

Arrêté Royal du 6 Février 1919

Art. 2. — Cette carte est obligatoire et est exigible à toute réquisition de la police. Elle doit être présentée à chaque changement de demeure dans la commune ainsi qu'à l'occasion de toute déclaration, demande de certificats et lorsqu'il s'agit d'établir son identité.

Art. 3. — Cette carte doit être renouvelée en cas de mariage et chaque fois que l'intéressé change de résidence, c'est-à-dire transfère sa demeure d'une commune dans une autre.

Les cartes détériorées par l'usage doivent être remplacées ; il en est de même des cartes des personnes dont la physionomie ne répond plus à la photographie.

Art. 4. Les personnes non munies de leur carte d'identité et d'inscription aux registres de la population et celles qui, ayant changé de résidence, auront négligé de la renouveler, sont passibles, conformément à l'art. 6 de la loi du 2 juin 1856, d'une amende qui ne peut exéder 25 frs.

ROYAUME DE BELGIQUE

COMMUNE DE SERAING

CARTE D'IDENTITÉ

et d'inscription

aux registres de la population

The cover of the small green identity papers which were faked for John by the Belgian resistance.

Observation : Quiconque modifie le texte ou remplace la photographie sur la présente carte. s'expose à des peines correctionnelles

Bastin
Nom
Albert, Georges, Félix
Prénoms
Etat civil Célibataire
Nationalité belge
né à Tilleur
le 3 Mars 1914.
Dessinateur
Profession
Résidence précédente
Seconde résidence
Inscrit Vol. 140 Fol. 128
Rue de Boncelles N° 82
le 12 Février 1942
C. R. n°

N° 13820
Signature du porteur :
A Bastin
Taille : I mètre .... cent.
SERAING, le 12 Février 1942
L'Officier de l'Etat civil (ou son délégué)

Demeures successives à SERAING

RUE	N°	D^on	Date

Vol. Fol.

Voir suite au verso.

The fake identity papers claim John is a Belgian named Albert Georges Felix Bastin. The photograph shows him in the civilian clothes the locals have provided for him.

“Mme Marchoul and Julia, her daughter, obtained some English books and one well-meaning friend of theirs brought along a pair of dumb-bells with which he hoped we would exercise every morning. Strange to say, we took his advice.”

Then the identity cards were delivered. They were brought to the house by Josef, an important official in the escape organisation, a few days after the men arrived at Mde Marchoul’s.

When he left he said he would be back the following Friday with working cards.

They, too, would be under John’s new identity, Albert George Felix Bastin, a dessinateur or draughtsman.

However, Josef was not to return.

Chapter Five

The Line Is Broken, May 28 to July 3

The night before he was to come back Josef was arrested by the Gestapo and the escape organisation went into what John Evans described as a "mild panic".

Two men came to the house and talked hurriedly with Mme Marchoul who then turned to the airmen and said they were being taken away immediately to a new hiding place.

John and Doug Lloyd scrabbled together their scanty possessions into little parcels and headed back to the same tram car. It was again packed full of German soldiers. The frightened airmen and the Wehrmacht rubbed shoulders, one terrified, the other largely uninterested in their fellow passengers.

Then one turned towards Doug and gestured for a match.

"He nearly had heart failure to find a Jerry addressing him," said John. "But he had the presence of mind to hand over a box without saying anything."

They left the tram in a suburb of Liège called Herstal and were taken to a garage.

"This had been used all day as a sort of dispersal centre for all the airmen, who like ourselves had been hurriedly evacuated from their previous houses."

The Americans who had been staying at the tailor's shop were among those hidden there as the Belgians tried to ensure that all their regular safe houses – the ones Josef could possibly give away under torture – were clean.

John, Doug and Robbie had had a less frightening escape than their colleagues from across the Atlantic.

They had been on alert since Josef, who had been due back the previous night, did not turn up.

At 5pm their worst fears were realised. They were staring out the window when a car screeched to a halt outside and five Gestapo men got out.

They came straight into the house and grabbed the tailor and his wife.

As the state policemen began to fire questions at the old man, the Americans pushed each other through the skylight onto the flat roof. They moved quickly and quietly to hide behind a chimney.

But even from their hiding place the Americans could hear the cries as the Gestapo carried out a brutal and swift interrogation of first the tailor and then his wife. Both were beaten. Tables and furniture in the house was thrown down and glass and china was broken.

The sounds of the destruction got nearer until one of the Gestapo men pushed open the skylight and looked out across the roof.

Luckily for the Americans he did not make a thorough search. Neither the tailor nor his wife had given any information away either, despite the threats and violence.

When the Americans had finished their story, the airman each drank down a glass of beer. It was just quick refreshment before the next stage of their dangerous journey.

John and Doug's new hiding place would be in the little village of La Prealle, just outside Liège. They would be sharing it with two of the Americans, Seattle-born Ken Griesel, the 1st pilot on a Liberator, and Alvis D Roberts, his bombardier, from Fort Worth, Texas. They had been shot down over northern Holland in March.

It was now May 28.

The new house was situated in the main street of the village.

"When we arrived there it was late evening and all the villagers were sitting outside their houses enjoying the last moments of sunshine," remembered John. "We were stared at a great deal, much to our embarrassment, and felt ourselves to be very conspicuous when we entered the house.

"It must have looked rather suspicious too as the house was owned and occupied by a middle-aged widow who lived by herself."

The new landlady was introduced to them as Mme Delchef. Her late husband had been a Belgian Army officer. He had died the previous Christmas. She hated the Germans intensely.

"Her dearest possessions were a couple of machine guns and a number of revolvers with plenty of ammunition which she kept under the tiles on her roof," said John. "She showed them to us one day and said that she was looking forward to the time when she would be able to use them fighting for the White Army against the Boches."

Louise Delchef went out to work every day and in the evening always brought back a small sack of white flour from a private mill which she helped to run. "White flour was just like gold and the bread that she used to make with it was very nice indeed," said John. "We were thankful for this bread as the black sticky stuff had begun to turn our stomachs.

"The remainder of our diet consisted mainly of potatoes and cauliflower or preserved beans. The ex-mayor of the village who knew of our presence there occasionally sent in a piece of black market meat – but this was not very often.

"Strawberries and cherries became quite plentiful towards the end of June and we ate such large quantities of both that once again our stomachs were upset."

Despite the danger of discovery, life could be tedious.

"During the daytime when Mme Delchef was out we occupied our time by playing cards or reading," John said. "The Forces programme on the BBC was on all day but of course we couldn't turn it up very loud."

Being in the centre of the village, the house would have regular visitors.

"Those people who knew we were in the house always rang the front bell four times, so that if during the day the bell was run once or twice we had to keep very quiet and usually one of us went upstairs and looked out of the window to see who it was," said John. "Doug and I occupied the front bedroom and Ken and AD the back one. Mme Delchef slept on the couch downstairs.

"One morning about nine o'clock the bell rang and she went to answer it. It was an official from the German labour office who went around finding out who was eligible to be sent to the Reich to work. We could hear him asking various questions in French to which Mme Delchef gave adequate replies.

"He was standing in the passage and saw her bed made down on the couch and asked why she slept downstairs. Her reply was that she had been troubled with her knee and that the doctor had told her that on no account was she to climb the stairs. Luckily he swallowed this."

On the morning of June 6 the men were lying in bed when Mme Delchef came rushing upstairs, the words tumbling out of her mouth about the landing at Normandy.

"She was crying for joy and flung her arms around each of us in turn. We were hardly less excited and immediately rushed out of bed, ran downstairs and switched the radio to the BBC.

"Sure enough, the great day had arrived. We felt very happy indeed and were convinced that our day of liberation was not far off.

"But we had to wait two and half more long months for that day."

In some ways the tension was now heightened. The British and Americans seemed so near but also so far away. Danger certainly remained closer and John and his friends were a long way from liberation, although they allowed themselves time to hope and celebrate.

"Nevertheless we often did get on each other's nerves and occasionally quarrels would start," said John. "The strain was quite considerable and we were longing to get away and try our luck on our own – especially after D-Day.

"We thought of some fantastic schemes for getting back to England but in the end our commonsense prevailed.

"But it was very difficult living in this house for six weeks and getting nowhere seemingly. If only we could have gone out for walks it would have helped to relieve the monotony, but of course that was out of the question.

"We did however become very firm friends in spite of our many England versus America arguments."

Mme Louise Delchef, who risked her life to run a safe house for downed airmen seeking help from the Comète Line.

Chapter Six

We regret to inform you...

Back home John's family would have given anything to know he was alive, even though he remained in danger.

On the day he and his crew went missing, 158 Squadron's commanding officer Wing Commander Calder wrote a letter to John's father at the family home, 'Noddfa', Main Street, Goodwick.

"It is with the greatest regret that I have to write confirming the news given in my telegram of today that your son, Flight Sergeant John Haydn Evans, has been reported missing from an operational sortie against Hasselt on the night of 12/13th May, 1944," he stated.

"The aircraft of which your son was pilot and captain took off at 21.56 hrs on 12th May, since when nothing has been heard. There is, of course, a possibility that the crew may have landed safely, but it is too early yet to expect any news of such an eventuality. Should I hear anything I will communicate with you immediately."

He concluded: "May I, on behalf of myself and the squadron as a whole, extend to you our sincere sympathy and understanding at this anxious time." He later sent the family a photograph of their son and his crew.

Three days later the squadron wrote to say it had collected John's personal effects from his room, the Sergeant's Mess and the locker rooms. The items had been sent to the Standing Committee of Adjustment, RAF Central Depository, Colnbrook, Slough. A Post Office Savings Bank book and £15.10.1 was also being stored. (A list of John's belongings was later sent to the family, including a chrome cigarette case, a grey pullover, three black ties, one Leg Junior camera in brown leather case, two coat hangers and three books.)

On May 20, a Charles Evans, of the Casualty Branch of the Air Council, Oxford Street, London, wrote to express his regret to Mr Ben Evans that his son was missing.

"This does not necessarily mean that he is killed or wounded, and if he is a prisoner of war he should be able to communicate with you in due course," he stated. "Meanwhile enquiries are being made through the International Red Cross Committee and as soon as any definite news is received you will be at once informed."

1588/C.452/102/P1.

No.158 Squadron,
ROYAL AIR FORCE.

13th May, 1944.

Dear Mr.Evans,

It is with the greatest regret that I have to write confirming the news given in my telegram of today that your son, Flight Sergeant John Haydn Evans, has been reported missing from an operational sortie against Hasselt on the night of 12/13th May, 1944.

The aircraft of which your son was Pilot and Captain took off at 21.56 hrs. on 12th May, since when nothing has been heard. There is, of course, a possibility that the crew may have landed safely, but it is too early yet to expect any news of such an eventuality. Should I hear anything I will communicate with you immediately.

It is desired to explain that the request in the telegram notifying you of the casualty was included with the object of avoiding his chance of escape being prejudiced by undue publicity in case he was still at large. This is not to say that any information about him is available, but is a precaution adopted in the case of all personnel reported missing.

I am enclosing a list of the names of the next of kin of the rest of the crew, with their relationship. It is contrary to Air Ministry policy for me to let you have their addresses, but should you wish to write to them and send me the letters, sealed and addressed, under cover, I will forward them.

Your son's personal effects are being collected and will be sent to the Standing Committee of Adjustment, Colnbrook, Slough, for onward transmission to you in due course. If you should wish to make any enquiry regarding your son's effects, will you please write to the Effects Officer R.A.F.Station, Lissett, East Yorkshire.

May I, on behalf of myself and the Squadron as a whole, extend to you our sincere sympathy and understanding at this anxious time.

Yours sincerely,

Wing Commander, Commanding,
No. 158 Squadron, R. A. F.

Mr.B.Evans,
Noddfa,
Main Street,
Goodwick, Pembrokeshire.

Immediately after John and his crew failed to return from the mission to Hasselt, 158 Squadron's Wing Commander Calder wrote to break the heartbreaking news to John's family in Goodwick, Pembrokeshire.

An enclosed leaflet entitled 'Advice to the Relative of a Man who is Missing' warned the family about news from unreliable sources such as "the enemy's broadcasts" of prisoners' names. "They are often misleading, and this is not surprising, for the object of the inclusion of prisoners' names in these broadcasts is not to help the relatives of prisoners, but to induce British listeners to hear some tale which otherwise they could not be made to hear. The only advantage of listening to these broadcasts is an advantage to the enemy."

The names of all those who have lost their lives, been wounded or reported missing would appear on official casualty lists and be published in the Press, said another leaflet. "Any premature reference in the Press to those reported missing may jeopardise their chances of evading capture, if they have survived without falling into enemy hands."

John's photograph finally appeared in the Fishguard County Echo on May 25, 1944, under the headline 'Missing Airman'. The story said simply that he was "missing after air operations". The photograph published with the story was taken during his army days.

On May 30, Lissett's Methodist Chaplain Joseph Parker wrote to express his sympathy in the family's "hour of distress". "But may I add that there are quite good hopes that he and his crew may have baled out and are safe, as many of our boys are who are reported missing from time to time," he wrote. "Let's hope so at all events, and pray that the time may soon come when he and all the splendid fellows who are now in enemy hands may return home once more."

Mr Evans responded: "I gratefully acknowledge your kind and sympathetic letter which was a great comfort to us in our distress. We can only hope for the best and pray to God that he is safe and that we shall have good news before long as it is a very great anxiety for all of us as a family."

On a purely practical basis, the RAF Benevolent Fund had written to Mr Evans a week after John went missing to say the family could continue to cash orders from John's order book "for a period". John, like many other airmen, had been making contributions to his family from his pay. Shortly afterwards, his parents were informed by the Air Ministry that if John continued to be missing the seven shillings a week payment could continue until November 9, 1944.

Strangely, John's family would learn something about the Halifax crew before John himself. On August 4, the Air Ministry wrote to state that "although no definite news of your son has come to hand, a report regarding certain of the occupants of the aircraft has been received from the International Red Cross Committee. This report, quoting German information, states that "Flight Sergeant FJ Tait and Flight Sergeant VG Colledge, members of your son's crew, were captured on the 13th May 1944."

158 Squadron
158S/C.452/102/P.1.

CONFIDENTIAL

CREW	NEXT OF KIN
658281 Flight Sergeant JOHN HAYDN EVANS Pilot	Father :- Mr. B. Evans
136357 Flying Officer JOHN BRYAN DANIELS Navigator	Father:- Mr. W.H. Daniels
CAN J.24485 Flying Officer WILLIAM ANTHONY ROBERTSON Air Bomber	Father:- Mr. J.J. Robertson
1585587 Sergeant DOUGLAS ALAN LLOYD Wireless Operator	Father:- Mr. H.E. Lloyd,
AUS426826 Flight Sergeant VIVIAN GRAHAM COLLEDGE Air Gunner	Father:- Mr. J.C. Cólledge
AUS426928 Sergeant FRANCIS JOSEPH TAIT Air Gunner	Father:- Mr. W. Tait
1604551 Sergeant LESLIE ERNEST BOARD Flight Engineer	Mother:- Mrs. E.B. Board

NOTE TO NEXT OF KIN : In order to avoid delay when writing to the Unit, please address all letters to 'The Commanding Officer'.

13th May, 1944.

PLEASE SEE BACK

This confidential RAF crew list shows the names of John and his crew, together with their next of kin.

Telephone No. Gerrard 9234
Trunk Calls and Telegraphic Address: AIR MINISTRY, LONDON.

AIR MINISTRY,
Casualty Branch,
~~Adastral House,~~
77, Oxford Street,
~~Kingsway, W.C.2.~~
London, W.1.

P417201/1/P.4.A.2.B.

20 May, 1944.

Sir,

I am commanded by the Air Council to express to you their great regret on learning that your son, Flight Sergeant John Haydn Evans, Royal Air Force, is missing as the result of air operations on 12th/13th May, 1944, when a Halifax aircraft of which he was pilot set out to bomb a target at Hasselt, Belgium, and was not heard from again.

This does not necessarily mean that he is killed or wounded, and if he is a prisoner of war he should be able to communicate with you in due course. Meanwhile enquiries are being made through the International Red Cross Committee, and as soon as any definite news is received you will be at once informed.

If any information regarding your son is received by you from any source you are requested to be kind enough to communicate it immediately to the Air Ministry.

The Air Council desire me to convey to you their sympathy in your present anxiety.

I am, Sir,

Your obedient Servant,

Charles Evans

B. Evans, Esq.,
Noddfa,
Main Street,
Goodwick,
Pembrokeshire.

The Air Ministry contacts John's family to show its "great regret" that John is missing.

ADVICE TO THE RELATIVE OF A MAN WHO IS MISSING

In view of the official notification that your relative is missing, you will naturally wish to hear what is being done to trace him.

The Service Departments make every endeavour to discover the fate of missing men, and draw upon all likely sources of information about them.

A man who is missing after an engagement may possibly be a prisoner of war. Continuous efforts are made to speed up the machinery whereby the names and camp addresses of prisoners of war can reach this country. The official means is by lists of names prepared by the enemy Government. These lists take some time to compile, especially if there is a long journey from the place of capture to a prisoners of war camp. Consequently "capture cards" filled in by the prisoners themselves soon after capture and sent home to their relatives are often the first news received in this country that a man is a prisoner of war. That is why you are asked in the accompanying letter to forward at once any card or letter you may receive, if it is the first news you have had.

Even if no news is received that a missing man is a prisoner of war, endeavours to trace him do not cease. Enquiries are pursued not only among those

The families of missing airmen were sent leaflets warning about enemy propaganda and advising on how to deal with the press in Britain.

MISSING AIRMAN

We publish above a photograph of Flight-Sergt. Pilot John H. Evans, Noddfa, Main Street, Goodwick who as reported in our last issue, is missing after air operations. He served in the Army for two years prior to joining the R.A.F., and the photograph was taken when he was in the former service

May 25, 1944, and the Fishguard County Echo, John's hometown newspaper reports that he is missing. The photograph shows him in army uniform.

Noddfa
Main Street
Goodwick
Pembs
3rd June 1944

Dear Sir

I gratefully acknowledge your kind and Sympathetic letter which was a great comfort to us in our distress. we can only hope for the best and pray to God that he is safe and that we shall have good news before long as it is a very great anxiety for all of us as a family

Kindest Regards
Yours Truly
B. J. Evans

John's father, Ben Evans, responds to one of the many official letters of regret and describes the family's distress and anxiety.

TELEPHONE: GERRARD 9234
Extn. 3800

Any communications on the subject of this letter should be addressed to :—
THE UNDER SECRETARY OF STATE,
and the following number quoted :— P.417201/1/44/P4.Cas.B4.
Your Ref. ....

AIR MINISTRY
(Casualty Branch),
73-77, OXFORD STREET,
W.1.

4th August 1944.

Sir,

I am directed to refer to the letter dated 20th May 1944 from the Department notifying you that your son, Flight Sergeant John Haydn Evans, Royal Air Force, was reported missing as the result of air operations on the night of 12th/13th May 1944 and to inform you that although no definite news of your son has come to hand, a report regarding certain of the occupants of the aircraft has been received from the International Red Cross Committee.

This report, quoting German information, states that Flight Sergeant F. J. Tait and Flight Sergeant V.G. Colledge, members of your son's crew, were captured on the 13th May 1944.

I am to add an expression of the Department's sympathy with you in your anxiety, and to assure you that you will be informed of any further news received.

I am, Sir,
Your obedient Servant,

for Director of Personal Services.

B. Evans, Esq.,
Noddfa,
Main Street,
Goodwick,
Pembrokeshire.

The Air Ministry keeps its promise to John's family to provide any news of their son or his crew. The new information, which has come through the Red Cross, is that two of the crew are prisoners of war. There is no information on John. At the time this was written he was being moved to a hunter's cabin near Porchuresse.

Chapter Seven

Into The Ardennes and More Danger, July 3 to August 4

On the night of July 3 a member of the escape organisation arrived at the house with urgent news. The town was getting too dangerous, but the forests of the Ardennes provided good cover.

"Liège was getting too hot and it seemed that many houses in the district were being searched for young men avoiding forced labour," said John. "Consequently, we were to be at the garage in Herstal at 7am and would be taken away in a lorry."

Once again they packed their few belongings and left the house at 6.30am.

"It was particularly dangerous to be seen on the streets now as the Germans had, since D-Day, developed the habit of sending out patrols to pick up any young men they could find.

"Therefore Mme Delchef led us through all the back streets until we finally reached the garage.

"There were six other airmen there when we arrived – all Americans.

"The plan was that we would ride in the back of a closed lorry, tucked down out of sight, with one man going ahead on a motorcycle to see if the Gestapo were stopping vehicles and as soon as he saw trouble to double back and head the lorry off in another direction.

"He was stopped four times altogether, but was allowed to proceed as his papers were in order. They showed that he was a good Nazi collaborator.

"Each time that he was stopped he managed to get back in time to warn the lorry driver.

"Once clear of Liège it was not so dangerous, and after about three hours travelling we arrived at our destination."

The new billet was a fairly large house in the village of Beffe, close to the tourist centre of La Roche. It was run by a couple named Vincent and Marie-Ghislaine Wuyts-Denis.

Vincent was originally from Brussels and Ghislaine – as John always knew her - from the Ardennes. They had been living in the capital until 1943 when the

Germans began rounding up all the young men for forced labour in Germany. Vincent and Ghislaine decided to move to the Ardennes: "A clandestine existence was much more preferable to having to work in Germany," said John.

Once there, they were approached by the Resistance to see if they would be willing to join the Comète Line, an organisation working to smuggle shot down Allied airmen back to England. They willingly agreed to help and became landlords of the house in Beffe.

Only a small trusted group knew what went on in the house in Beffe.

"They were the Burgomaster of Beffe, the local forester and an English lady married to a Belgian farmer who lived a few miles away. This lady used to bake bread for us – always done at night away from prying eyes – and Vincent would then go and fetch it on his bicycle.

"Food was always a problem but they worked wonders with what was available. It had to be brought to the house in small quantities anyway as large deliveries would have aroused suspicion in the village."

Added John: "We felt much freer here as there didn't seem to be a German within miles of the place. Every night at midnight Vincent or Louis or Bob would take us for walks through the woods and sometimes we would bathe in the river.

"In the mornings we would peel potatoes and saw wood and do any other jobs that needed doing and then in the afternoon we would settle down to a session of bridge. There were only four of us who could play and as we were all pretty keen there was never much difficulty in forming a school."

John admitted life in this quiet part of the Ardennes became "quite a pleasant existence" and that most escapees even "rather enjoyed it", but they were still evaders and not everyone coped.

"There were one or two who just couldn't adapt themselves and became very discontented," he said.

"One of these – he was a rear gunner and came from North Wales – could stand it no longer, just doing nothing and getting nowhere, as he called it, so one night he decided to go off by himself.

"This was very dangerous. If he was caught, he could possibly be forced to divulge information putting the organisation in danger.

"He left with a compass and a map, a loaf of bread and some tobacco. We never saw or heard of him again. I do not know what happened to him."

The rest stayed put and lived out a life "very smoothly" until all threatened to go wrong at the end of July when the Germans launched a massive raid on the village.

Although John and the others were not the target, but a house on the other side of the church where four members of the Armée Blanche were hiding, they found themselves in great danger as the violence erupted.

"The men must have been informed on for one morning, about 4am, a lorry load of Germans arrived in the village and stopped on the green right outside our house," remembered John. "They then ran to the house being occupied by the Armée Blanche men and broke the door down.

"One of the men fired at the German officer and wounded him and he and another were promptly mown down by a machine gun.

"A third was running away through the fields behind the house when he was shot. The fourth was hiding in a cellar beneath the house and the Germans did not find him.

"After they had killed all the occupants, as they thought, the soldiers burned the house down and went away. But before they left the officer warned the Burgomaster that if any more recalcitrants were found then the whole village would be burned to the ground. All these details were recounted to us by Vincent who had obtained them from the Burgomaster himself."

When the Germans arrived John's hosts went into a panic. Vincent and Ghislaine shook the airmen awake and pushed them quickly out through the back door, pointing them to the nearby woods.

"There was clearly a state of some panic but it was obvious that the Germans did not know of our presence as they made no attempt to enter our house," said John. "It was also clear that the person who had denounced the young men would have done the same for us had he been aware of our existence there.

"It was decided that it was too dangerous to return to the house and we would have to remain in the woods until plans were made to take us elsewhere.

"We stayed in the woods four days and nights before we were on our travels once again."

John described the last night in the woods - July 28, 1944 – as "one of the most miserable that I have ever spent".

He remembered: "A tremendous thunderstorm broke at about 12.30am and so heavy was the downpour that it was impossible to find any shelter anywhere. We were all soaked through to the skin.

"Our clothes, blankets and palliasses were all wet through and, worst of all, our tobacco and cigarettes were completely destroyed.

"There was nothing for it but to sit there in misery until daylight and then when the sun came up we managed to dry out our clothes."

By morning they were ready for some good news.

"A priest dressed in full clerical garb arrived with the news that six bicycles had been brought to a nearby village and that they would be used to enable six of us to leave on the next stage of our journey. He would be taking us to another camp.

"We drew lots and I was one of the lucky ones."

The priest, who they later came to know as Abbé Arnaud, gave them detailed instructions about the distances to be kept, what to say if they were stopped and what to do in the event of punctures and breakdowns. They walked down to the village, were given a bicycle each and set off.

"The going was fairly easy until we got to La Roche and after that it was all up hill and down dale. Some of the hills were very steep indeed. We stopped once to eat sandwiches that had been prepared for us by Ghislaine.

"The distance between each pair of cyclists had to be quite considerable so that no suspicion would be aroused. Therefore when we came to crossroads one of the foremost cyclists would have to stop and point the way that the guide had taken and then take up his position at the end.

"Gradually we all became more tired and were in need of rests more frequently.

"One of the larger towns that we passed through was St Hubert where a number of German soldiers were to be seen in the street and where it was even more important to maintain our distances in order to prevent suspicions that we were all travelling together. Even so I felt very conspicuous and thought that hostile eyes were on me as I went through the town.

"There was a café somewhere on the route which was owned by one of the men in the organisation and where we were to get some refreshments."

They arrived at the café at about eight in the evening. They were exhausted.

"The man in charge brought us two bottles of beer each but we drank them so quickly that they did us more harm than good."

In fact, one of the Americans, Alvis D Roberts, collapsed on to the table and was unable to continue any further. A decision was taken to leave Roberts behind and he would follow on a few days later after he had recovered.

The rest found themselves in the hands of a new guide. The priest left and a young man called Louis Vanlierde took over.

"He was aiming at getting us to our destination that night and to do so it was necessary to pass through the small town of Paliseul by 10.15pm at the latest because the curfew came into effect at 10.30pm and it was dangerous to be seen

Vincent Wuyts who, together with his wife, Marie-Ghislaine Wuyts-Denis, ran the Comète Line operation in the Ardennes town of Beffe.

Marie-Ghislaine Wuyts-Denis.

This is the house in Beffe where Vincent and Marie-Ghislaine hid John for most of July 1944. This photograph was taken after it was badly damaged during the Germans' Ardennes offensive – and the Battle of the Bulge - later that year.

George W. Dople - 149 Main Street, Latrobe. Pennsylvania
THEODORE S. Simmons - 124 WEST ELM STREET Lima, Ohio U.S.A.
HAROLD E. ASHMAN - Route 5, GREENVILLE, OHIO
Milo. E. BLAKE - 1656 GROVE ST. SAN FRANCISCO, CALIFORNIA
William P. ELSBERRY - Post ENGINEERS, CAMP BLANDING FLA.
David R. Talbott - Bristol, Maryland - U.S.A.
ALVIS D. ROBERTS - {FORT WORTH, TEXAS, U.S.A.} {1008 EAST JEFFERSON}
Alan R. Willis, 146 Hawley St. Binghamton, New York
WINANS C. SHADDIX DOUBLE SPRINGS, ALA. U.S.A.
Henry H. Gladys. 216 Liberty Ave. Monessen, Pa U.S.A.
J H EVANS: NODDFA GOODWICK PEMBROKESHIRE S WALES G. BRITAIN
K. C. GRIESEL 3227 39th AVE. S.W. SEATTLE. 6, WASH., U.S.A.
D.A. LLOYD: "GREENMANTLE", 130. PRIORY LANE ROEHAMPTON. LONDON. S.W.15.
R. MORETON 236 DAWLISH DRIVE ILFORD ESSEX England
Fred A Tuttle 521 No. Ben Wiley St. Santa Maria Calif.
C. WESTERN. 22 STUART ROAD HEAVITREE. EXETER. ENGLAND
C.L. Weymouth Abbot, Maine U.S.A.
Russell Geck's 10 CONNECTICUT Ave. FREEPORT, New York
G.E.H. FLATHER 277 NORRISTHORPE LANE HECKMONDWIKE Yorkshire
KEVIN J. DOYLE 2068 W 6th AVENUE VANCOUVER BC CANADA.
RA WEEDEN 38 FELSBERG ROAD - BRIXTON HILL - LONDON SW1 ENGLAND
DICK KINDIG - INDIANA - SOUTH BEND USA.

Vincent and Marie-Ghislaine kept a list of the airmen they had helped and buried it in a bottle in the garden so that they could keep in contact after the liberation. John's is the eleventh name on the list.

on the streets after that time."

They struggled on but it became increasingly evident that they were not going to make that deadline.

"Ken Griesel and another American called Hank Gladys were in a bad way. At one point we had to wait on top of a hill for Ken. He came staggering up, pushing his bicycle, and as soon as he reached us and stopped, he fell flat on his face on the grass verge – out for the count."

Griesel's friends struggled to revive him and by then it was 10.30pm and the group had to find somewhere to spend the night.

"About half a mile down the road we came to a rather dilapidated looking house with an even more dilapidated looking shed next to it," said John.

Vanlierde knocked at the front door and there was an anxious wait until an old man came to one of the upstairs windows. Louis called to him, asking if they could stay the night in his shed. But the old man appeared suspicious, seemed to think the men were up to no good and would not give permission.

The men were tired and desperate though. They ignored him and went over to the shed to break down the door.

They went inside, stumbled to the ground and went to sleep. John and the airmen were apparently too exhausted to worry as to whether the old man who owned the shed would call the authorities but John learned later that Louis stayed awake all night with his revolver in his hand in case the farmer decided to turn informer.

At about 7.30 in the morning the group got back onto their bikes. They could see the old man looking at them from behind a curtain, but he was too scared to do or say anything.

They eventually passed through Paliseul and arrived at a farm. The farmer was a member of the organisation and was expecting them. He made them food which they ate quickly, they were ravenously hungry, and then they went to the barn and slept until late afternoon.

When they woke, they found that another guide, a young man named Albert, had arrived to take them away to a camp deep in the woods. They walked for about two hours until they eventually arrived at a cabin which had been made out of pine trees and tarpaulin.

There were already three occupants there: Flight Lieutenant Bob Morgan, a Canadian Mosquito pilot; Lieutenant Sam Schlickhorn, an American and pilot of a Liberator and Second Lieutenant Maupin, another American who had crash landed his Thunderbolt.

“They were very glad to see new arrivals and once again we spent a long time swapping experiences,” said John.

Hardworking Albert spent the day on a farm and every evening he would bring the fugitives a sack filled with bread, milk, potatoes, butter, tobacco and any other spare food that he could lay his hands on.

“We were now nine so it took quite a lot of food to keep us satisfied. Sam was the cook and we managed very well on two meals a day. For breakfast we always had a bowl of porridge and then about 7pm we had a plate of boiled potatoes with bread.

The camps and safe houses formed a chain down which the evasion line hoped to move escapees on their way to freedom in a neutral country or, during the second half of 1944, behind the battlefront which was moving away from the Normandy beaches.

After only five days, the priest came with six other airmen who then took over the camp. John and the others were supplied with a bicycle each and they were once more on the move. The next camp was fifteen miles away and, while it was run on much the same lines as the previous one, its cabin was much better. It had been a hunters’ cabin in peace time and boasted windows, a fire place and a table. The new arrivals built their own beds with trees, wire and ferns, and so “lived in comparative luxury” from August 4 until August 28.

Chapter Eight

'The Plumber', and Only Yards from Capture, August 4 to 28

At Porchuresse the Comète Line was run by Emile Roiseux with the help of a man named Raymond. They lived in the village but looked after the airmen in the nearby wood.

John Evans came to know Emile as a "remarkable man" although, as with the other members of the escape line, the airmen would not know their full stories until after the war and the danger had passed.

"He was brave if sometimes foolhardy and had a deep hatred and contempt for the German forces occupying his country and an even deeper hatred and contempt for those of his fellow countrymen who became collaborators with the occupiers," said John. "He was French by birth but at the start of the war he was working as a plumber in Brussels and after the occupation he became an active member of the Resistance in that city.

"He was known in the Comète escape line as Le Plombier and one story in particular illustrates how close he came to being captured.

"He went to a house in Brussels to meet some of his fellow Resistance colleagues. He did not know that the house had just been raided by the Germans and many of his friends arrested.

"When he entered he was confronted by two Gestapo officers with guns cocked and at the ready. Fortunately he was carrying his plumber's tools and with great presence of mind he told them that he had called to the house to deal with a plumbing problem.

"One of his arrested colleagues confirmed that he had called for a plumber the previous day and said that he had no idea who Emile was.

"The Gestapo were eventually convinced that he was not known to those who had been arrested and allowed him to go to the basement to attend to the supposed problem.

"He was allowed to leave finally and immediately began telephoning everyone he knew to warn them of what had happened."

After that scare Emile had had to leave Brussels for the Ardennes but he continued his Resistance activities. Earlier in 1944 the Comète Line organisation had come to him to set up the camp near Porchuresse.

The organisation provided Emile with money to feed the airmen and John and the others would collect it in sacks.

"Each night after dark three or four of us would go through the woods into the village to the house where Emile lived," explained John. "There were always plenty of volunteers for this job as it meant that we could listen to the news in English."

And there were plenty of reasons to try to listen to the BBC. The Allies had been busy fighting their way inland from the beaches of Normandy, taken Caen on July 9, St Lô on July 18 and, when on July 26, General Patton's US Third Army broke out of the beachhead and overran Brittany, the battle of Normandy became the battle for France. By the time Paris fell at the end of August, the Germans were in retreat towards the Siegfried Line, leaving behind half a million casualties – dead or captured - on French soil.

"There was great excitement at this time as the Allies were beginning to push out from Normandy," recalled John. "On that day Emile brought up a special bottle of wine to celebrate."

The good news from the war helped make for a relaxed feeling around camp.

"Life went along quite pleasantly at this camp," remembered John. "There was a river about a mile away and we used to go down there most afternoons for a swim. We occupied ourselves during the rest of the day by making model aeroplanes or just sunbathing.

"The weather was glorious all through the month and we became quite sunburnt. When it became dark we would light a log fire, gather our chairs around it and just talk. Sometimes there would be a little community singing – very softly, of course."

One day, while the group was chatting, Emile mentioned that there was a little house belonging to a Rexist – a Belgian collaborator - about two miles from the cabin.

The Rexist and his family were in Brussels at the time. "Someone suggested that we should go and break into the house and take anything which might prove of some use to us."

All the group thought that was a great idea and soon after the five airmen, Emile and another man named Jean set off by night through the trees. They had a lot of difficulty finding their way through the darkness but eventually got out beyond the wood to the house.

They broke a pantry window and climbed inside. The Rexist's house was a wooden chalet and, according to John, was "beautifully done out inside". The walls were panelled, the furniture appeared very expensive and the carpets were plush. "The owner must have spent a great deal of money on it," said John.

And then the intruders – each with an empty sack - set about it

"There was plenty of stuff to steal and we weren't long in filling our sacks with crockery, wine, food, clothing, fishing tackle and anything else which caught our fancy," said John. "One chap discovered a cuckoo clock and another, a javelin.

"The two Belgians went around the rooms with axes and smashed up the furniture, wash basins, and then poured varnish over the floors. They just seemed to go mad and gave the impression that they hated the collaborators more than the Germans themselves. The Belgians regarded the Rexists as traitors.

"The booty came in very handy in the cabin as we were very short of some things, particularly crockery."

They had one scare while at the camp and that came towards the end of August.

Jean was walking through the woods with food for the camp. On the way he had to pass through a large clearing where the trees had been cut down and were being hauled away at various times for the Germans. By a stroke of bad luck on that day there were five German soldiers standing in the middle of the clearing - and Jean didn't notice them. He walked merrily out of cover causing the Germans to spin around.

They shouted to him to halt. He turned, saw them and knew he was in trouble.

He quickly dived into the trees and began to run.

One of the Germans unslung his automatic and fired after him. Jean felt a bullet wing the side of his side but he carried on, crashing through the undergrowth.

About 800 yards away the men in the cabin jumped alert at the rat-a-tat of the shots echoing through the woods. Birds screeched through the trees and the airmen struggled to work out what was happening.

Suddenly Jean arrived at the cabin, blood streaming from his head. "Get out quickly," he said. "Germans."

A plan had been put in place at the camp for such an emergency, although the airman had hoped never to have to use it. They had found another well-sheltered place not far away.

Everyone got up quickly and sharply and made it out of the cabin in what John called "orderly fashion" - all except Sam who made a dive through the window. And that was the last the others saw of him for three days.

Fortunately, it was also the last they would see of the German soldiers. They made little attempt to follow Jean far and had not seen the cabin.

"After about two hours Emile came up from the village and said that they had gone away," said John. "We then all trooped back to the cabin."

Chapter Nine

The Sounds Of Liberation, August 28 to September 9

When word came that all the airmen in the Porchuresse camp were to move to the south, it meant saying goodbye to Emile. They had developed a bond with him and so parting was a sad affair.

The new guides took them on a march through the forest at night.

"Our instructions were to walk in two files on each side of the path and to make as little noise as possible in order to minimise the risk of unwelcome attention," remembered John. "We were now in the hands of the Armée Blanche – the equivalent of the French Maquis – and they were all heavily armed."

Halfway through the journey the guides stopped and gave the airman food and drink; then they continued south.

Eventually they reached the area around Bohan-sur-Semois, a small town near the French border. This, they knew, was somewhere near the advancing Allied armies. The plan now was simple: to lie low in the woods there and wait for the liberators to arrive.

Hiding, though, as John remembered was getting more and more difficult.

"Doug Lloyd and I were now in a party of 25 or 30 evaders and four or five Belgians who were wanted by the Germans for a variety of reasons," he said. "We set up a primitive camp in the middle of dense woods near Bohan.

"There was nowhere to sleep except above ground with whatever shelter one was able to improvise from trees and bushes.

"Food was a problem especially as we were now such a large contingent but a few villagers including Alexis Henry who was a Belgian customs officer brought us what they could."

Even from the isolation of the woods they occasionally got a sense of how the war was progressing.

"There was a road not too far away and we could hear the rumble of German vehicles as they retreated along it," he said. "Occasionally Allied fighter planes would appear and attack the retreating convoys and when this occurred the Germans would scatter into the woods alongside the road but never far enough to encounter us.

"Some of the German transport was horse drawn and quite often during these

With liberation near at hand the RAF, American and Canadian airman of the secret camp in the woods at Bohan-sur-Semois pose with the local Belgian resistance workers. John Evans is second from the right in the back row. The woman in the centre is Comète Line guide, Yvonne Bienfait.

This photograph of Bohan-sur-Semois was taken before the war but clearly shows the bridge that was badly damaged as the American's liberated the town. John waded across the river to get to the Americans.

attacks horses were killed and were then left on the roadside and this proved to be a welcome source of additional food for the villagers and for us too. They would come out at night and cut off as much meat as possible and some of it was brought to the camp where it was soon cooked and eaten providing a very acceptable supplement to our meagre rations."

After five days in the camp they were visited by an excited villager who said the Germans had gone and the Americans were near at hand.

"We hurriedly gathered our few belongings and ran down to the village," John said. "Every house had a British or American flag flying from the window and the people were beside themselves with joy and welcomed us with open arms."

Within a short time, John and the others found they had just one more hurdle to clear for freedom.

"The main bridge across the Samois had been blown up by the retreating Germans and when we reached it an American armoured vehicle could be seen on the opposite side of the river," he said.

"Our joy was overwhelming. We waved and shouted at the soldiers, took off our shoes and socks and rolled up our trousers and waded across. The occupants of the American vehicle could hardly believe their eyes and ears when our unkempt mob approached them speaking English."

This amazing photograph shows the damage to Bohan-sur-Semois and the river John and the others waded across to meet the advancing Americans soldiers.

While travelling towards Paris the Belgian resistance fighters and the Allied airmen stopped to meet the advancing American GIs. John Evans is not in this photograph but the man smoking a cigarette and holding a guitar is Ken Griesel, the American Liberator bomber pilot with whom he had been hiding. The man in the long white coat and beret is a local leader of the Belgian White Army, the resistance. The woman in the centre of the photograph is Yvonne Bienfait, of the Comète Line. The man standing on the right, who seems to be holding a bunch of flowers, a gift perhaps from a grateful local villager, is Alvis D Roberts, another American airman who had been hiding with John Evans.

Everyone hurried to explain who they were and the Americans broke out the K rations before taking the ragged looking visitors back to their field headquarters.

"There we were questioned and then taken to another command centre where further interrogation took place and arrangements made to take us to the American HQ in Paris," said John.

"We travelled in an open lorry, partly through the night and all the time passing a continuous stream of American tanks and other army vehicles travelling in the opposite direction.

"All the French towns and villages that we passed through were bedecked with French, British and American flags and the happiness of the people everywhere was unbelievable."

The American HQ in Paris was the Hotel Meurice in the Rue de Rivoli. During the occupation it had been the headquarters of the German military governor of the city.

John Evans and the other liberated airmen were taken from Belgium by the resistance following the liberation and, travelling towards Paris in the back of an open lorry, watched the Allied forces pressing towards Germany. Here, the group encounters an American tank and jeep near a railway tunnel. An abandoned pillbox is to the left of the photograph.

Another photograph taken from the back of the lorry while on the way to Paris. This photograph shows US Stuart tank in a town in the French Ardennes.

The last governor had been Generalleutnant Dietrich Choltitz, who days earlier had faced a difficult choice while defending the city. The Communist-led resistance cells had risen up against his garrison on August 19 and Hitler had ordered the city destroyed, famously asking his staff: "Is Paris burning?"

However, Choltitz had ignored Hitler's orders to burn the city and on August 25 the advancing Americans and the resistance overcame the few soldiers and collaborators who were defending the French capital. Around 10,000 German soldiers surrendered.

The following day the leader of the Free French forces, Charles de Gaulle, entered the city and addressed Parisians: "Paris! Paris outraged! Paris broken! Paris martyred! But Paris liberated!"

Paris was free, although there were remnants of Nazi resistance: at one point a sniper even opened fire on de Gaulle from a hotel, but he was not hit.

John and the others arrived in the city on September 5 and, although the city had been spared real damage, it still bore some scars of battle.

"When we arrived at the Hotel Meurice signs of the fight that had taken place a few days previously between the French resistance and the Germans were apparent everywhere – burnt out vehicles, bullet scarred walls.

"The Americans treated us with great courtesy and consideration. After the usual questioning Doug Lloyd, who had been my constant companion since we were shot down, and I were kitted out in GI uniforms and given bedrooms in the hotel.

"The change in our circumstances was dramatic. Food was now plentiful and we slept in beds with proper sheets. Champagne which had been found in the hotel after the Germans left was also made available so a good time was had by all during the few days that we were there."

This photograph was taken on September 5, 1944 near the Hotel Meurice in Paris, shortly after the city was liberated. It was taken by a member of the Belgian resistance who was escorting John and others to the hotel. Flags from the buildings to welcome the liberators, while most of the vehicles in the street have been burnt out in the recent fighting.

The picture was also taken near the Hotel Meurice, Paris, on September 5, 1944, shortly after the city was liberated. While a man inspects a burnt-out German army vehicle, other residents of the city attempt to go about their normal lives.

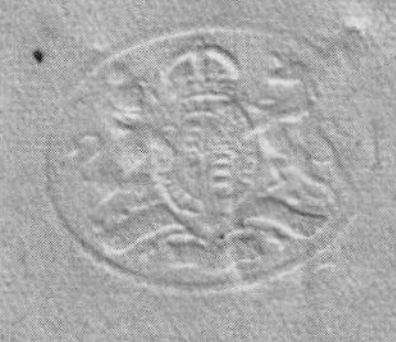

158S/C.452/102/P1.

No.158 Squadron,
ROYAL AIR FORCE.

21st September, 1944.

Dear F/Sgt.Evans,

I was very glad to receive your letter of 18th September. Many congratulations on your return. I had received no official notification of your return, although news had come through that F/O Daniels and Sgt.Board are back and Sgt.Colledge and Sgt.Tait are prisoners of war.

Your log books will have been sent to Air Ministry (Archives) and your new unit will recover them for you.

I am writing to the Secretary of the Caterpillar Club applying for membership on your behalf and you should get the card shortly. I am told there is a five months delay in supplying the badges.

Yours sincerely,

W J Weller. S/LDR.

~~Wing Commander~~, Commanding,
No. 158 Squadron. R. A. F.

F/Sgt.J.H.Evans,
Noddfa,
Goodwick,
Pembrokeshire,
S.Wales.

158 Squadron responds to a letter from John revealing that he has finally returned safely to Britain.

Chapter Ten

Home

After a taste of life in liberated Paris, John Evans and his wireless operator Doug Lloyd finally heard that arrangements had been made for their return to Britain. They returned on September 9 – four months after they had left.

After arriving at Northolt they were taken to the Air Ministry for debriefing and then were allowed some very welcome leave. Firstly, they went together to Doug Lloyd's parents' home in Roehampton. From there, Mr Lloyd kindly telephoned Mr Fielding, a neighbour of his sister Enid in Port Talbot to pass on the news that he was back in England and was safe and well.

"Both my sisters Enid and Mair came to speak to me and a more emotionally charged conversation could not be imagined," recalled John. "It was so wonderful to talk to them again and they of course were ecstatic.

"My phone call to my sisters has been spoken about so many times down through the years. Not many people had phones in those days but Doug's father had one and when he rang through to my sister Enid's neighbour in Margam whom I knew had a phone, luckily Mair happened to be there at the time. He went and told Enid that her brother was on the phone and she naturally enough thought it was my brother Doug.

"It is difficult to describe what happened when she heard my voice - disbelief, then joy and tears, so much so that they were almost unable to talk for a little while and then it was all of a jumble before I was able to tell them what had happened. It was an extremely emotional experience for us all. I knew that Enid had been expecting a baby and she was so happy to tell me that he had arrived when I was in Belgium and that he had been named after me - John David Setchfield, who later worked for BBC Wales.

"They then telephoned the police station in Goodwick to pass on the news to my parents and their reaction after many months of worry can only be imagined."

The next day John travelled down to Port Talbot to spend a few days with Enid before going on to Goodwick where his father was waiting for him at the station. "It was a truly memorable home-coming and I was welcomed by everyone I met," John said. "The interest in me and my recent experience was widespread and I had to tell and retell my story many times."

NORTH GALLERY

ROYAL AIR FORCES ESCAPING SOCIETY

DEDICATION OF A MEMORIAL PLAQUE
AT
THE ROYAL AIR FORCE CHURCH OF
ST. CLEMENT DANES

SUNDAY, 21st JUNE 1981 AT 11 A.M.

The Congregation is requested
to be seated by 10.30 a.m.
Dress: See over

A.
Back
1.

John's invitation to the dedication of a Royal Air Forces Escaping Society plaque at the RAF church in London. It pays tribute to all the men and women of occupied countries who helped 2,803 aircrew of the RAF and Commonwealth air forces to escape and survive during World War 2.

John now discovered that two other members of the crew, Flying Officer "Danny" Daniels and Sergeant Les Board had also returned home. Colledge and Tait remained prisoners of war.

Not surprisingly, when now given the choice between returning to Bomber Command or transferring to Transport Command, he picked the latter.

At the end of his leave he was sent to No105 OTU at Bramcote, near Worksop, where he renewed his acquaintance with the Wellington aeroplane.

It was time for a new crew now: Bill Briden, navigator and Dave Barrell, wireless operator. "Both were very experienced Warrant Officers and extremely efficient at their respective duties and we became a very happy team."

The training at Bramcote and its satellite airfield, Lindley, started on November 30, 1944 and lasted two months and John was soon confidently flying the Wellington once again.

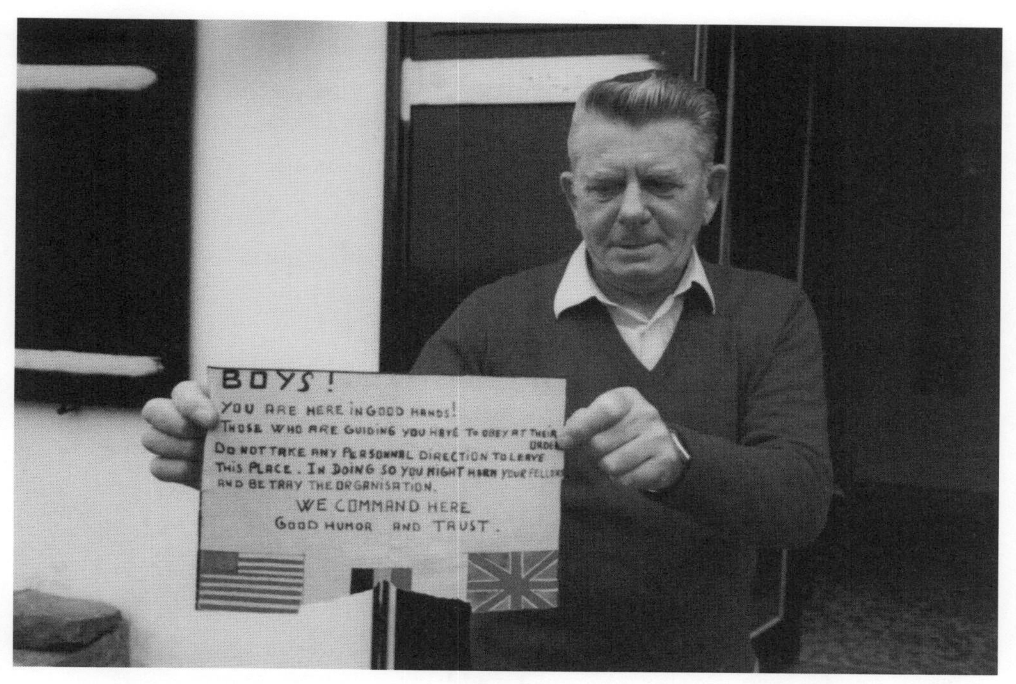

Emile Roiseux, the Comète Line's Le Plombier is pictured in October 1984, holding a notice which was on the wall of the hut in the woods at Porchuresse forty years earlier. It is written in slightly faltering English, but gets the message across. It states: "Boys! You are here in good hands! Those who are guiding you have to obey at their orders. Do not take any personnal direction to leave this place. In doing so you might harm your fellows and betray the organisation. We command here. Good humor and trust."

Things got even better when through a stroke of luck the crew was posted to No II Ferry Unit at Talbenny, near Broad Haven, in Pembrokeshire, a short although not always easy journey from Goodwick. John's hometown now not only offered the attraction of his family: while on leave straight after his escape from Occupied Europe, he had met a young woman named Jeanne and a "new life of great happiness started for me".

"I had only recently met Jeanne and was now able to spend many weekends at home with her, subject as they used to say to the exigencies of the service. But it did mean in effect that most of our weekends were free so the only problem was getting to Goodwick and back again which I managed by a combination of service transport, public transport and lifts from various kind friends."

Life at Talbenny was very different to bombing raids over occupied Europe, but it was still busy, beginning with trips to Llandow Airfield near Cardiff to collect aircraft.

"Our job was to fetch Wellingtons and Ansons (Mark XII), a small twin-engined monoplane similar in size to the Oxford, test them and fly them out to Blida in North Africa," explained John. "Flying the Wellingtons out was a

John Evans, pictured in January 2007, at his home near Nottingham. In the background is a painting of the Halifax 'Friday the 13th' which he had flown in May 1944. (Picture: Greg Lewis)

somewhat boring task as it involved a direct non-stop flight but Anson trips were much more interesting.

"They were completed in a series of stages or hops because of the limited full capacity of the aircraft. Our first stop was always Port Reith in Cornwall and the next was Rennes in Britanny. From there we went to Toulouse, then Istres, near Marseilles, and finally Elmas, near Cagliari, Sardinia, before crossing the Mediterranean to Blida, which was not far from Algiers.

"The whole of France had now been liberated so all the airfields were open to us.

"The Anson flights usually took three days so we had to stay overnight at least one of the stopping points. We were on our own, never pressed for time, and led quite a leisurely existence. To get back to England we had to be taken first to Maison Blanche, Algiers, which in those days was a big American air base, and then we had to persuade the authorities to give us a lift back to England on any Dakota - DC3 - which might be returning there with passenger space to spare.

"On landing at Lyneham or Bovingdon a phone call to Talbenny soon brought an Anson to fly us back to base."

John was at Talbenny from February 20, 1945 until July 12 when the Ferry Unit closed.

His final, job in the wartime RAF began when he became one of two staff pilots at No 4 Group Communications Flight based at Full Sutton in Yorkshire. The aircraft there were Oxfords, Proctors and De Havilland Dominies and the pilots' task was to fly senior staff officers from No 4 Group Headquarters to various destinations and then return.

"In effect it was a glorified air taxi service. Once again it was quite an easy-going existence apart from one incident which I see from my log book took place on November 27 1945.

"I had taken five passengers to Syerston airfield in the Midlands and on the return flight, after crossing the Humber, I found that the whole of South Yorkshire was covered in thick fog.

"I flew for some time in the general direction of Full Sutton but it became impossible to see the ground and the darkness too was not far away. I contemplated heading for Carnaby on the east coast where a massive purpose built runway existed to enable badly damaged bombers to land when returning home but without any chance of reaching base.

"FIDO facilities were also available at Carnaby: this was a war device for enabling aircraft to land by dispersing fog by means of petrol burners on the ground.

"Suddenly through the murk I made out the outline of an aeroplane on the ground and realised that I must be over an airfield."

John made a decision to land immediately. He braced himself.

"Continuing to circle, I eventually picked out a concrete strip which appeared to be part of a runway and, keeping this in sight, I lowered the undercarriage and flaps and brought the plane in to land not knowing what part of the runway we were on," he said.

"I switched off the engines and applied the brakes but in no time at all the plane ran off the end of the runway into an area of soft earth.

"Fortunately no one was injured although the plane was slightly damaged.

"Five very relieved passengers and pilot were picked up by station transport and taken to flying control."

John had landed at Pocklington airfield, not far from Full Sutton to where he returned the next day.

Warrant Officer John Evans' war had effectively been over for some time. In May 1945 everyone celebrated as the conflict in Europe ended and in August came the Japanese surrender. More than 55,000 aircrew in Bomber Command had lost their lives.

Now, Britain began to demobilise its forces.

"My last day at Full Sutton was December 5 when I had to report to 4 Group HQ at Heslington Hall, near York, for final instructions," said John. "I was now entitled to several weeks demobilization leave and after spending Christmas at home reported to the appropriate centre at Uxbridge on December 27, 1945, for completion of the necessary formalities including the collection of my civilian clothing."

With his demob suit on, John looked back at his wartime career in the army and RAF as a "time of excitement and danger interspersed with occasional periods of boredom, but over all a happy experience during which I made many fine friends, some of whom, alas, did not live through it. Luck was on my side for which I am grateful."

It was time now to settle into civilian life again. After a brief period working for the Ministry of Agriculture in Haverfordwest John passed the examination for entry in HM Customs and Excise.

But his next big date was February 5, 1946, when he and Jeanne were married at Margam Abbey, Port Talbot.

All the time he remembered those who had come to his aid for the months he was in danger in 1944.

"After being shot down I am sure the possibility of being captured came into one's mind and it was purely a matter of luck as to how one evaded capture," he said. "If good fortune led you to a sympathetic person, as it did in my case, then the first dangerous hurdle was over. I cannot say that the possibility of being shot ever crossed my mind."

Chapter Eleven

Old Friends and Former Enemies

After the war John made a number of visits back to Belgium to link up with members of the evasion line who had helped keep him free of the Nazis.

He set off to track the people who helped save his life, travelling with his wife Jeanne, his brother Doug and Doug's wife Dorothy.

Doug, who had completed a full tour of operations in 10 Squadron and was awarded the Distinguished Flying Cross, went into civil flying after the war and became a flight manager with British Airways on Tridents and Tristars.

Doug took the wheel as they drove around Belgium.

Mijnheer and Mevrouw Buntinx, the farmers who took him in at first, were traced for John by Jaak Cardinaels, who as a teenager during the dark days of the war had arrived at the farm to interrogate him.

Jaak, who had then been the courier who took John and Robbie to Zonhoven, lived in Bree in Belgium until his death in 1993. In a letter to John in 1980 he recognised the way the war had connected them even though "we have met only a few moments". The man, who as a 14-year-old had joined the resistance and risked his life every day, added: "I, for myself, had forgotten the war. I didn't want to have any thanks or medals or something else because I thought I had nothing done (sic) but my duty."

John had met Jaak in 1980 in the home of René Jaspers – the Baron's helper - in Zonhoven and after that they remained in regular correspondence. Jaak tracked down a lot of information for John, including the exact spot where his plane crashed ("From some parts of the plane," he told John, "people made saucepans and cooking pots.")

John never got to meet Mijnheer Buntinx after the war - he had died in 1949 – and by 1980 all that remained of the farm was a barn.

However, John was reunited with his widow during a visit to Belgium in 1982 with Jeanne, Doug and Dorothy.

"We had a wonderful reunion in her house near Zonhoven and were introduced to a large number of her family including sons and daughters who as small children were seated around the farmhouse table when I arrived in 1944," he remembered.

"Sadly, she died before I could see her again but, according to Jaak, the priest at her funeral said that she told him how happy she was to have met me again before she died."

Shortly before the meeting and on learning her and her husband's name for the first time in November 1980, John had written to her: "I have never had the opportunity of thanking you for all that you did for me and my comrades in those dangerous days in 1944 so I would now like you to know how grateful we are. You were very brave people."

The Baron's two helpers, René Jaspers and Louis Wouters, both suffered for their work in the underground.

René, who was only 16-years-old during 1944, lived with his parents and family in Zonhoven.

When the escape line was infiltrated by the Germans in July 1944, René and M Biernaux, who had hidden Doug, Robbie, and John in his home in Hasselt, were arrested by the Gestapo and suffered appallingly.

René was taken to Breendonck concentration camp, near Antwerp, and then to Neuengamme concentration camp in Germany where ill treatment and near starvation almost killed him. Fortunately, he survived and was freed when the camp was liberated.

His health was broken, though, and he spent several years in a Swiss sanatorium before he was fit enough to return home to Zonhoven.

During his time in Switzerland he trained as a watchmaker and when he came home he set up in business as watchmaker and jeweller in Zonhoven. He married Juliette and they had four children. John and Jeanne visited the family a number of times and the Belgian family also came to Britain.

René died on December 17, 1992. On learning of his death, John wrote to René's wife Juliette: "My thoughts immediately go back to 1944, of course, when he became my friend for life through his courage and bravery in helping me and many others in spite of great danger to himself and to his family. I could never repay him for all that he did for me at that time when he risked his own safety and indeed his life so that we could evade capture. Sadly he suffered greatly because of the cruel treatment he received after he was arrested but he lived the rest of his life with pride in the knowledge that he did all he could for his country at the time of its greatest need. He was a great patriot and his country should be proud of him…So it is farewell to my dear friend, René. A man of exceptional quality. (Jeanne and I) are proud to have known him and will remember him for ever."

Louis Wouters worked for the Baron as a forester on the estate and when they had warning of René's arrest he and his family left home because of the danger. He remained in hiding until the arrival later that summer of the advancing British troops.

Louis, who also remained in contact with John, died in September 1999.

The good fortune of the brave Hasselt family - Florent, Olympe and Raymond Biernaux - and other helpers in the area, ran out shortly after they had hosted John, Robbie and Doug. The family had helped 53 airmen when the Gestapo and Belgian police knocked at their door early in August 1944. At the time they were hiding two Canadians, one of whom was wounded. They had tried to take them to Liège but a raid had damaged the electric current to the tram and they were forced to turn back.

"Two days later," wrote M Biernaux in a letter to John Evans immediately after VE Day, "I was advised that the line was broken."

The family decided to hold onto the two men and hope the Allies reached Belgian soon.

M Biernaux described what happened next in faltering English, but the story was harrowing.

"When I was arrested and been beaten five times of the Gestapo, without say a word," he stated. "I stay in the prison of Hasselt. My wife was beaten also and my son and Jack go also to prison.

"The 14 August (nine days later) my wife, Mrs Degueldre of the café and her daughter, we were all sent to the big prison of St-Gilles (Brussels). They leave all Brussels for Germany on 1 August and they reached Ravensbrück, one of the baddest camps of Germany.

"I alone remain to Brussels, with 1,500 other men and women to be shot, but the splendid advance of the Allied troops obliged the Germans to run away."

Florent Biernaux was able to escape on September 2, and tried to get out of the city by train. He reached as far as Muysen (Muizen) before turning back and eventually finding the Allies had reached the capital on September 3.

"What my wife, Mrs Degueldre and her daughter had suffered in Germany is not to tell you," he wrote. "They must work 12 hours every day, one week by daylight, one week by night. They receive only one cup of soup (hot water) and a piece of bread for a day.

"They came back 24 May (1944). My wife had lost 45 pounds in weight. You know her and you can't imagine how she is skinny now.

"We know nothing of my son. We know that Jack is death in Germany.

"When I came back to Hasselt, the 10 September 1944, I found my home completely plundered by Gestapo and other collaborators."

M Biernaux asked John to send him a photograph of the airman in "parade clothes" so they could put it on the mantelpiece of their home.

He added: "I hope that God will give us back my son Raymond and then we can begin again a new life."

Sadly, that was not to be the case. Raymond would never return home. Cecile Jouan's book Comète - Histoire d'une ligne d'evasion lists Raymond Biernaux as having died at Neuengamme concentration camp, near Hamburg, on March 3, 1945. He was 20.

After the war, John learned that the evasion line leader whom the men had all known as the Baron was actually Baron de Villengfagne of Kasteel Vogelsanck, near Zolder, Zonhoven.

By the time John and his family began visiting René and Louis in 1980 the Baron had been dead for four years.

"But René took us to see the castle which is a beautiful chateau type building alongside a lake. We were introduced to and had a long talk with his son who has succeeded to the title and the estate."

Vincent and Marie-Ghislaine Wuyts-Denis, said John, were "very brave people indeed". They helped more than twenty Allied airmen by hiding them in the large house in Beffe during 1944.

"We all wrote our names and addresses and the list was placed in a bottle by Vincent and buried in the garden of the house until the war was over when we returned to Beffe and recovered it from its hiding place," said John. It is a fascinating document, scrawled with many names including Evans, Griesel and Lloyd. Each airman has listed his home address too, so that R. Moreton, of Dawlish Drive, Ilford, Essex, is followed by Fred A Tuttle, of Santa Maria, California. Most entries come from all over the United States, while there are a few from Britain and one from Canada.

Interviewed many years later for De La Meuse à l'Ardennes Vincent and Ghislaine said they were never afraid during the occupation, despite the incredible risks they took. However, Ghislaine added: "As members of Comète, we had to be available at all times solely to help the evading Allies. That is why Vincent had to decline the offer to become a member of the Front de l'Indépendance. They must have taken us for lukewarm Belgians."

John lost contact with Vincent and Ghislaine for many years but discovered them again in 1980 at a little village called Cugnon on the river Semois in the Ardennes. The search had started with René Jaspers who found an elderly lady in Beffe who remembered them.

Vincent and Ghislaine then become very dear friends of John, Jeanne, Doug and Dorothy. Together they revisited Beffe and the surrounding area, and they were reunited in Britain too.

"One of our proudest moments is of the Bomber Command Association dinner at Grosvenor House, London, in 1983," said John. "During his speech Air Chief Marshal Sir Arthur Harries spoke about the brave people who helped to get his airmen back from enemy occupied territory and, knowing of their presence, asked Vincent and Ghislaine to stand up.

"The applause was overwhelming and later on so many people came to our table to be introduced and to speak to them and to obtain their autographs as well as to hear about the wartime exploits. It was a very emotional experience."

Another reunion involved Emile Roiseux, Le Plombier, who John describes as a "remarkable man".

"He was a man to whom all of us who were helped and sheltered by him owe more than we could ever repay."

After the war Emile and his brother set up a plumbing business in St Pierre-sur-Dives in Normandy.

John lost contact with him after the war but Vincent and Ghislaine helped bring them back together.

The first reunion took place in Bayeux in 1982 with John's family joining Emile and his wife Andrée for a tour of the D-Day landing beaches and various associated museums.

Two years later at Cugnon Emile was accompanied by his daughter Marie-Claire, who had been only about five-years-old in 1944.

"He took us on a nostalgic visit to the woods in Porchuresse and showed us the old route that was used to get to the hunter's cabin in 1944 and finally the cabin itself," said John.

"It had changed somewhat since then as it had been renovated and looked smaller than I remembered it.

"Also many of the surrounding trees had been cleared leaving a much more open area around the cabin. In 1944 it was well concealed by closely growing trees and high bushes."

During the same visit, Brussels hosted a reunion of the Comète Line.

There, John and his wife Jeanne met the priest, Abbé Arnaud, and Louis Vanlierde, the guides who took the airmen on the cycle ride from Beffe to Paliseul. One evening they gathered in a flat owned by Louis and his wife Christiane. The attendance was remarkable: Vincent and Ghislaine, the Abbé,

Emile, and John's brother and sister-in-law Doug and Dorothy.

"It was a unique occasion in that we were all there together with five people who had done so much for me in 1944 at great risk to themselves," said John.

"The talk and reminiscences went on well into the night. A truly memorable occasion."

Between 1977 and 1979, the BBC and BRT (Belgium) joined together to dramatise the story of the Comète Line in Secret Army. The programme, which starred Bernard Hepton, Angela Richards and Clifford Rose, regularly attracted 15 million viewers. Its technical advisor Group Captain William 'Bill' Randle CBE AFC DFM had himself been 'down the line' and over three series it paid a fitting tribute to the people who had protected John and others like him.

The RAF Church of St Clement Danes in London features a plaque to the French, Belgian and Dutch civilians who helped a total of 2,803 down Allied airmen evade capture during World War 2. It shows an airman with a male and female helper. A parachute can be seen in the background and the scene is criss-crossed by searchlights.

After the war John was reunited with some of his crew through the RAF Escaping Society and he met new friends through the organisation for shot down airmen, the Caterpillar Club.

He remains in touch with Bill "Robbie" Robertson and they still talk about the way they evaded capture all those years ago. The Canadian had been separated from John and Doug in Liège, and been sheltered by the then head of police in the town. John said: "I guess he saw the way things were going and did it as a kind of insurance against the time when inevitably the Germans would leave and his own record would be scrutinised. After the war 'Robbie' was asked by the authorities to testify to the fact that he had been sheltered by this man and his family." Robertson was liberated by the American army in early September 1944, returned to his native Canada, where he still lives.

Les Board was also sheltered by the organisation in Liège and would have been liberated about the same time as Robbie. He subsequently worked as an engineer. He died in 2005.

Doug Lloyd, who had shared much of the experience of evasion and survival with John, remained in the RAF and obtained a permanent commission. He died in 1988.

John was never reunited with his navigator "Danny" Daniels. He cannot be sure why. "There were many among us who inevitably wanted to put it all behind us and try to forget it all, but whether this was so in his case I just do not know," he said. "He certainly did not join the now-defunct RAF Escaping Society."

He never found out what happened to the two Australians, Dick Colledge and Frank Tait, who had been captured immediately after escaping the burning aircraft. "Efforts to trace them later on in Australia proved fruitless but a few years ago I was reliably informed that they had both died," he said sadly.

John's last raid had been the second on the town of Hasselt in consecutive nights. During the night of May 11-12, 1944 bombs had fallen in the centre of the town. Nine houses had been completely destroyed, and a church, hospital and the Béguinage – a collection of small buildings used by the Catholic church – had been damaged. A home for the elderly, the Zegershuis, was also heavily damaged. Seventeen elderly people from that home lost their lives.

On May 12-13, by the time the bombers returned to Hasselt and Leuven, the inhabitants of Hasselt had been evacuated, according to Wim Govaerts, and, although several houses along the Kuringse Steenweg were destroyed, no lives were lost. "Many bombs fell in the surrounding fields, and the actual target - the railway and station - were hardly damaged," stated Wim. "The loss of aircraft, including John's Halifax, was actually a high price which Bomber Command had to pay for this operation."

Looking back in 2007, John said: "During the time I was in Bomber Command I can truthfully say that the morality of what we were doing was never in question as far as I remember. We were fighting a cruel and ruthless enemy who was dangerously near our shores and, after the evacuation at Dunkirk in 1940, the only way this country could hit back for the next number of years was through Bomber Command.

"Hitler devastated many of our towns and cities including London, Coventry, Liverpool, Plymouth and many more with a huge loss of innocent lives. Sadly, the same thing happened in Germany when our response came and even when industrial targets were attacked there was inevitably loss of life among the civilian population.

"War is war and a very cruel thing it is when innocent people have to suffer so much. One remembers the crushing of Germany in 1945 with the Russians advancing from the east and the Allied armies from the west and the awful civilian suffering that ensued. Unfortunately we still see it going on in Iraq and Darfur and other places across the world. When will the world come to its senses about the futility of war, I wonder?

"I am well aware of the debate still going on about the validity and morality of wartime bombing but it is all very well discussing it with hindsight by people who were not there when the reality and the demands of that time were so very different.

"During the war Bomber Command lost 55,000 brave men and whatever the rights and wrongs of the campaign at least their heroism and self-sacrifice should be remembered and honoured. Sadly, we seldom hear much about it nowadays. Am I bitter? A little, perhaps. But there we are."

In 2003, for John's 84th birthday, his daughter, Judy, and son-in-law, Ira, bought him a trip in a Tiger Moth. Halfway through the flight the instructor allowed John to take the controls: it was 63 years since he had first taken the controls of a Tiger Moth for his first solo flight.

John lost his wife Jeanne in April 1998. The couple had lived for many years on the Wirral, where John had worked for HM Custom and Excise at Liverpool. After Jeanne's death John moved to Calverton, near Nottingham.

And what of Heinz Wolfgang Schnaufer, the man the RAF feared so much they dubbed him 'The Spook of St Trond', the man who sent John Evans and his crew rushing through the escape hatch of their bomber?

Promoted to Hauptmann the month he shot John down, he remained as Kommandeur IV./NJG 1 until November 1944, receiving the Eichenlaub and Schwerter (the Oak Leaves and Sword additions to his Knight's Cross), and moving with the unit when it retreated back to Germany.

He shot down his 100th aircraft on October 9, 1944, and received the Brillanten (the Diamonds grade of the Knight's Cross) from Adolf Hitler.

He was still only 22. He became Kommodore NJG 4 at Gutersloh and was promoted to the rank of Major.

Astonishingly, his greatest exploit was still to come. On February 21, 1945, he destroyed nine RAF heavy bombers in one day, two in the early hours of the morning and seven in a nineteen minute frenzy of courage and destruction that evening. According to Peter Hinchcliffe, author of The Other Battle, post-war research suggests there may even have been a tenth victim that day.

By the time Nazi Germany surrendered and Schnaufer was taken prisoner by the British in May 1945 at Eggebek, in Schleswig-Holstein, Schnaufer had 121 victories. (The tail fin of his aircraft, which displays his kills, is kept at the Imperial War Museum, London.)

It would be another fifty years before John Evans learnt that this was the man who shot him down.

But, they would never get to meet for real.

With the war over, Schnaufer had returned to Calw to take over the reins of a family wine business left by his father who had died in the war.

In July 1950, while travelling in a sports car near Bordeaux in France on a trip to buy wine, a lorry pulled out without warning. This time Schnaufer's lightning-fast, fighter pilot reactions could do nothing to help him.

Two days after the crash Schnaufer died in hospital. He was 28.

John discovered it was Schnaufer who shot him down through his former colleague and bomb aimer, "Robbie" Robertson. He had previously never tried to find out whose hands were on the controls of the night-fighter which shot him out of the sky in May 1944.

When he was finally told, Schnaufer's death left John with unanswered questions. If John had had the opportunity to track down the Luftwaffe ace who had tried to kill him he would have done so as eagerly as those who had saved his life.

"I would have been interested in meeting Schnaufer after the war and I don't think I would have felt any animosity towards him," he explained. "After all he was doing his best for his country and we were trying to do the same for ours. Isn't it the tragedy of war that people who would normally live in friendship and harmony are thrown into deadly conflict with each other?

"I think I would have asked him whether there was any single tactic that contributed to his phenomenal success as a night-fighter bearing in mind that his radar operator, Rumpelhardt, and gunner, Gansler, were both very experienced and remained with him for a long time and must have contributed greatly to his success.

"Secondly I would be interested to know if he ever flew over the UK, perhaps as an intruder. Intruders were active at one time in attacking bombers as they approached their bases in England after an operation.

"Finally I would love to have known his true opinion of the Nazi regime. We know from the attempt on Hitler's life in 1944 what many high ranking officers thought and for which they paid with their lives. There must have been many others who thought similarly but kept it to themselves."

John knows now he will not get an answer to these questions but he has spent time researching the pilot.

"I have a book called Luftwaffe Aces by Franz Kurowski, translated from the German, and one chapter is devoted to Schnaufer," he said. "It ends with an account of the road accident in which he was killed and the final sentence reads, 'An anonymous French truck driver had accomplished what hundreds of the enemy had failed to do during the years of war'.

"It is a shame that he had gone through all that he did and was then killed like that. But his good luck had finally run out."

Author's Note

This book is based on notes started by John Evans soon after the Second World War and on interviews with John between September 2006 and February 2007. My thanks, in particular, go to him and his family.

There are many websites which have a great deal of detail about the Comète Line. These include John Clinch's http://home.clara.net/clinchy/neeball.htm and www.escapelines.com, and the website of Le Courrier Comète Kinship Belgium Association. Other sources of information and help are credited in the text;

I must thank Wim Govaerts, of Belgium, in particular, for his information on Schnaufer and the Hasselt raid.

I first learned about John from a fascinating feature by Andy Smart in the Nottingham Evening Post and from an article in the Western Telegraph.

My wife, Moira, was my partner in writing the book. My thanks go to her, and also to Leo and Mary for their comments, interest and help.

Thanks always to Clive, Mary and Mark.

The Author

Greg Lewis is a freelance journalist.

He has written for a number of publications, including The Times, Private Eye and The Big Issue Cymru, and regularly works for ITV Wales in Cardiff, where he lives.

He is the author of A Bullet Saved My Life, a biography of Spanish Civil War veteran Bob Peters.

Lfd. Nr.	Typ	Datum	Uhrzeit	Ort	Höhe	Zeugen	Bemerkungen
40	Lancaster	9.5.44	3.34	bei Grandreng (30 km SW Chalerol)	2400 m	Oblt. Schnaufer, Ofw. Gänsler	(mit Oblt. Schnaufer) brennender Absturz nach 2 Angriffen anerkannt Nr. 435/44
41	– " –	13.5.44	0.36	5 km ONO Hasselt	2300 m	Uscha. Holtermann, Fp.Nr. 32 158 Rottenfhr. Brindöpke – " –	(mit Oblt. Schnaufer) brennender Absturz nach 1 Angriff anerkannt Nr. 456/44
42	– " –	– " –	0.44	Londerzeel 8 km W Mecheln	2800 m	Oblt. Schnaufer, Ofw. Gänsler	– " – anerkannt Nr. 435/44
43	Halifax	– " –	0.48	Hoogstelen (6 km NW Turnhout)	1500 m	– " –	– " – anerkannt Nr. 435/44
44	Lancaster	22.5.44	1.34	3 km SO. Moll	6200 m	– " –	– " –
45	– " –	– " –	1.51	10 km S. Herenthals	5800 m	– " –	– " –
46	– " –	23.5.44	1.23	bei Neerpelt	6000 m	– " –	– " –
47	– " –	– " –	1.36	bei Brecht (22 km NO. Antwerpen)	5500 m	– " –	– " –
48	– " –	25.5.44	1.15	3 km NW Eindhoven	2500 m	– " –	– " – schwache Gegenwehr
49	– " –	– " –	1.18	2 km NNW Tilburg	2500 m	– " –	– " –
50	– " –	– " –	1.22	1,5 km W Goirle (7 km SSW Tilburg)	2500 m	– " –	– " –
51	– " –	– " –	1.25	zwischen Dongen u. Tilburg	2500 m	– " –	– " –

This picture shows a page from a Leistungsbuch *relating to Schnaufer's radio/radar operator Fritz Rumpelhardt. A* Leistungsbuch *was a kind of performance book – not a log book – in which the time, altitude and location of a 'kill' was noted. Line 41 records the crew's meeting with John Evans' bomber 2,300 metres above Hasselt at 00.36am on May 13, 1944.*

Luftwaffe ace Heinz Wolfgang Schnaufer.

From left to right: Oberfeldwebel Wilhelm Gänster, Major Heinz Schnaufer, Leutnant Friedrich Rumpelhardt.

Standing in front of their JU88G-1, from left to right: Gänster, Schnaufer, and Rumpelhardt. When this photograph was taken neither Gänster or Rumpelhardt had received their Knights Cross. Gänster's was awarded on the 27th July 1944, and Rumpelhardt's on the 8th August.

Luftwaffe ace Heinz Wolfgang Schnaufer.